CYCLL
GUIDE 2025

Experience the Island's Energetic Atmosphere

Donald V. Middleton

Copyright © 2025.

All rights reserved. No part of this publication may be reproduced, distributed, or transmitted in any form or by any means, including photocopying, recording, or other electronic or mechanical methods, without the prior written permission of the publisher, except in the case of brief quotations embodied in critical reviews and certain other noncommercial uses permitted by copyright law.

Table of contents

Discovering the Cyclades
- Welcome to the Islands
- Geography & Climate
- Cultural Heritage
- Suggested Itineraries

Trip Planning
- Getting there and around the Island
- Accommodation Guide
- Sustainable Travel
- Shopping Tips

Must-Visit Islands
- Santorini
- Mykonos
- Naxos
- Paros
- Milos
- Ios
- Syros
- Sifnos
- Amorgos
- Tinos
- Serifos
- Folegandros

- Koufonisia
- Andros
- Antiparos

Culture & Traditions
- Historic Sites & Museums
- Local Festivals
- Village Life
- Artisan Workshops
- Hidden Treasures
- Outdoor Adventures
- Family Activities
- Nightlife & Entertainment

Food & Drink
- Local Cuisine
- Best Tavernas
- Wine & Spirits
- Cooking Classes

Practical Information
- Packing Guide
- Budgeting Advice
- Emergency Contacts
- Greek Phrases

conclusión

Discovering the Cyclades

Welcome to the Islands

My journey to the Cyclades Islands remains one of the most memorable chapters of my travels. It wasn't just the stunning landscapes or the warm Mediterranean waters that made it unforgettable, but the deeper connection I developed with the place and its people.

It all started with an unassuming flight from Athens to Santorini, the island everyone knows for its whitewashed buildings, blue-domed churches, and breathtaking sunsets. But for me, the magic didn't come from the typical tourist attractions. Instead, it unfolded when I stepped off the plane, ready to experience the islands on my own terms.

Santorini greeted me with the usual sights: the famous caldera, the sweeping views over the Aegean, and the bright blue sky that seemed to stretch forever. But I quickly learned that there was so much more to this place. As I wandered through the narrow cobblestone streets of Fira and Oia, I made an intentional choice to escape the crowds and seek something different. That's when I stumbled upon the island's lesser-known treasures.

On my first morning in Santorini, I set out early before the sun became too intense. The streets were quieter then, offering a sense of serenity that I didn't expect. As I explored the island, I found myself drifting away from the usual tourist hotspots. Instead of heading straight to the famous viewpoint for the perfect sunset shot, I took a detour to a small, almost hidden cove I had read about in a local guidebook. There, the water was calm, almost still, reflecting the sky like a mirror. It was one of those rare moments when you realize the true essence of a place isn't in the crowds or in the photos people take—it's in the quiet moments, the parts of the island that people don't often notice. I spent hours there, listening to the soft waves, letting the salty breeze refresh my mind.

After a few days in Santorini, I hopped on a ferry to Mykonos, another well-known gem in the Cyclades. Mykonos is often painted as the party island, but I was determined to look beyond that image. As soon as I stepped onto the island, I was greeted by the sight of narrow alleys and whitewashed buildings draped in bougainvillaea. The island was more than just a place for nightlife; it was a place steeped in history, culture, and art.

One of my favorite moments was spent wandering through the island's quieter areas, far from the bustling town center. I found a small, family-run restaurant tucked away on the outskirts of Mykonos Town, with a view of the sea. The owner, an elderly woman named Maria, welcomed me with a warm smile and a plate of the freshest seafood I had ever tasted. As we sat and chatted, I learned about the history of the island, her family's long-standing connection to the land, and the changing tides of tourism that had shaped Mykonos into what it was today. Maria's stories were more captivating than any guidebook description, and it was in these intimate moments that I truly understood the island's soul.

While Mykonos was stunning in its own right, I found myself longing for a change of pace. That's when I decided to head to Naxos, a larger island known for its lush landscapes and rural charm. It was a stark contrast to the crowded streets of Santorini and Mykonos. Naxos was where I felt most connected to the Cyclades' natural beauty. The island's verdant valleys, mountain villages, and ancient ruins made it a place where I could unwind and slow down.

I rented a car and drove inland, far from the well-trodden paths that most tourists take. The further I went, the more I found myself surrounded by olive groves, vineyards, and wildflowers. The landscape was so vibrant, it felt like stepping into another world. Along the way, I discovered small, forgotten villages where time seemed to stand still. In one such village, I met a local farmer named Kostas, who invited me into his home for a cup of Greek coffee. His humble abode was adorned with old farming tools, and his family's story was written into the walls of the house. Kostas shared his experiences of growing up on the island and how the pace of life had changed with the rise of tourism. I realized that these personal interactions were what truly brought the Cyclades to life for me.

As I explored Naxos further, I found myself at the Temple of Apollo, one of the island's most iconic landmarks. But even here, I didn't feel like I was just a visitor; I felt as though I was walking through history. The massive marble doorway, known as the "Portara," stands as a testament to the ancient civilization that once thrived on this island. As I stood there, watching the sun begin to set behind the columns, I reflected on how the island had been a crossroads for civilizations for thousands of years. It wasn't just a place to take photos; it was a living, breathing monument to history, culture, and endurance.

After spending several days on Naxos, I moved on to Paros, another island in the Cyclades that I had heard much about but hadn't yet explored. Paros was a place that seemed to balance tradition and modernity in the most beautiful way. The island's charming villages were full of narrow streets lined with cafes and shops selling local art. The beaches were less crowded here, offering the perfect setting for reflection and relaxation.

One afternoon, I rented a bike and rode along the coast, stopping at small villages along the way. In one of these villages, I met a young artist named Elena who had moved to Paros from Athens to escape the fast-paced city life. She had opened a small art gallery in the heart of the village, where she showcased her paintings and sculptures inspired by the island's landscapes. Elena and I spent hours discussing art, life, and the pull of the Cyclades. For her, the islands were more than just a place to live—they were a source of endless inspiration, a place where the light, the colors, and the tranquility of the landscape seemed to bring out the best in her creativity.

By the end of my time in the Cyclades, I had come to realize that these islands weren't just about beautiful beaches, historical sites, or picturesque villages. They were about the moments in between—the quiet conversations with locals, the time spent away from the crowds, and the sense of connection that develops when you allow yourself to truly experience a place. The Cyclades, with their mix of history, nature, and culture, had given me more than just memories. They had given me a deeper understanding of the world, one that could only be gained through meaningful experiences and personal connections.

Geography & Climate

The Cyclades Islands, a group of 56 islands scattered across the Aegean Sea, are an iconic destination in Greece known for their stunning landscapes, charming white-washed buildings, and rich history. These islands are part of the larger South Aegean region and are famous for their unique geographical features and Mediterranean climate, which make them an attractive choice for travelers seeking both natural beauty and cultural heritage.

Geographically, the Cyclades are located between the mainland of Greece and Turkey, forming a crescent shape with islands such as Santorini, Mykonos, Naxos, Paros, and Ios among the most well-known. The islands vary greatly in size, ranging from the larger islands like Naxos, which covers about 429 square kilometers, to smaller ones like Delos, which is uninhabited but holds immense archaeological significance.

The topography of the Cyclades is primarily rugged, with steep hills and valleys that provide breathtaking views of the Aegean Sea. While each island has its unique landscape, many share the characteristic of steep cliffs along the coastline, making for stunning vistas at almost every turn. The islands also feature rocky terrains, with many being devoid of large forests, which gives them a stark, almost barren beauty. It's this dramatic landscape, combined with the clean white buildings and blue domes of the architecture, that creates such a visually striking contrast.

The climate of the Cyclades plays a significant role in their appeal as a summer destination. The islands are bathed in Mediterranean sunshine for much of the year, offering visitors dry and hot summers, with temperatures often rising above 30°C (86°F) in July and August. The warm weather creates the perfect environment for beach-goers, with beaches stretching across the islands offering clear blue waters perfect for swimming, sunbathing, and watersports.

In contrast, the winters are mild and rainy, particularly in the months of December and January. While it rarely dips below 10°C (50°F), the cool and wet season can make the islands feel quiet and peaceful, as fewer tourists venture out during this time. However, this off-season period is perfect for those who enjoy exploring the islands without the usual summer crowds.

One of the key natural features of the Cyclades is the powerful wind that often sweeps through the islands, particularly in the summer months. The "Meltemi" winds, which blow from the north, can reach speeds of up to 7 Beaufort, especially in July and August. These winds, while they may occasionally make the sea rough and challenging for sailing, are also responsible for keeping the air fresh and the temperatures from becoming stifling. The winds also contribute to the characteristic whitewashed architecture, as they help to keep the buildings cool.

The islands' geography makes them particularly attractive for outdoor activities. Hiking is popular on many of the islands, and for those who enjoy a more active exploration, trails that wind through the hills and valleys are numerous. On Naxos, the island's highest peak, Mount Zeus, reaches 1,004 meters, offering panoramic views of the Aegean and the surrounding islands. Hiking to the summit provides both a physical challenge and a rewarding experience with unmatched views. Paros also offers scenic trails, especially around the Paros Park area, where walkers can enjoy coastal routes and explore wildlife-rich environments.

Each island's coastline varies, with sandy beaches on some islands and rocky coves on others. Paros has many beautiful beaches like Golden Beach and Kolymbithres, both renowned for their crystal-clear waters. Meanwhile, on Mykonos, the beaches are livelier, with numerous beach bars and restaurants lining the shores. However, quieter spots can be found in more remote areas of the island, such as the northern beaches of Mykonos like Agios Sostis. Santorini, although famous for its caldera and cliffs, also has some unique volcanic beaches like Red Beach and Kamari, where visitors can swim and relax surrounded by dramatic landscapes.

On the smaller islands, there is often an opportunity to explore more hidden and less commercialized locations. The island of Ios, for example, while well-known for its vibrant nightlife, also offers serene spots like Manganari Beach, which remains more peaceful despite its beauty. Folegandros, another quieter island, is known for its cliffs and stunning views, perfect for those looking for a tranquil escape.

The Cyclades also have a strong connection to history and archaeology, making the islands not only a destination for relaxation but for cultural exploration. One of the most famous historical sites in the Cyclades is Delos, a UNESCO World Heritage Site, located near Mykonos. Delos was once a powerful religious and commercial center in ancient Greece and is now an archaeological park that is open to the public. The island is home to a variety of ancient ruins, including temples, houses, and marketplaces, all of which offer fascinating insights into the island's storied past. Visitors to Delos can take guided tours to learn about its history, as well as marvel at the impressive collection of statues and mosaics that have been uncovered.

Santorini, while renowned for its dramatic landscapes, also has significant historical and archaeological sites. The ancient city of Akrotiri, often referred to as the "Pompeii of the Aegean," was preserved by volcanic ash after the eruption that devastated the island thousands of years ago. The well-preserved ruins of Akrotiri offer a glimpse into the advanced civilization that once flourished on the island, with frescoes, pottery, and architectural structures still intact. The Museum of Prehistoric Thira, located in Fira, further enhances this experience, housing many of the artifacts discovered at Akrotiri and providing valuable context for visitors.

Beyond these larger attractions, the islands also have a wealth of smaller, more intimate sites that reflect the daily lives of their residents throughout history. The island of Naxos, for example, is home to the Temple of Demeter, a beautiful and less crowded site that offers both historical significance and scenic views. This temple, dedicated to the goddess Demeter, is located in a lush valley and is a peaceful place for reflection.

The small village of Pyrgos on Santorini offers visitors a chance to step back in time and experience traditional island life. This charming village, located on the slopes of the island's central peak, is less commercialized than some of the other villages and has managed to retain its authenticity. Visitors can stroll through its winding streets, explore its historic churches, and visit the Venetian castle at the top for an incredible view of the island.

Another must-visit is the medieval village of Chora on Folegandros. With its narrow streets and whitewashed houses, Chora offers an opportunity to immerse yourself in traditional Greek island life. The village's beauty lies in its simplicity, with no major tourist attractions, but rather an abundance of local tavernas and small shops selling handmade goods.

The combination of these varied geographical and cultural elements creates an island-hopping experience in the Cyclades that is truly one-of-a-kind. Whether you're hiking to the top of a mountain, visiting ancient ruins, or simply relaxing on a sun-drenched beach, the islands provide something for every type of traveler. The mix of natural beauty, ancient history, and modern-day charm ensures that a trip to the Cyclades will be as enriching as it is visually stunning.

Prices for accommodations, meals, and activities vary widely depending on the island and season. For instance, in Santorini, expect to pay higher prices for hotels, particularly in Oia or Fira, where a mid-range hotel can range from €100-€300 per night. On islands like Naxos or Paros, prices are more affordable, with mid-range hotels averaging between €60-€120 per night. It's also worth noting that many attractions, like the Akrotiri archaeological site, charge an entrance fee of around €12, while the archaeological site of Delos has a fee of €12 as well. For those interested in exploring the islands by ferry, prices typically range from €10-€50, depending on the distance between the islands.

Cultural Heritage

The Cyclades are rich in cultural heritage, offering a diverse and fascinating tapestry of ancient ruins, traditional villages, and a thriving contemporary arts scene. The islands, with their long history, showcase a blend of Greek, Venetian, and Ottoman influences, creating a unique atmosphere that draws visitors from all corners of the globe. The cultural wealth of the Cyclades is reflected in everything from the monuments and art to the lively festivals and traditions that are still alive today. Exploring these islands is an opportunity to step back in time while simultaneously experiencing the vibrant culture that continues to thrive.

In the Cyclades, each island tells its own story through its architecture, archaeological sites, and the everyday life of its people. The island of Delos, for instance, stands as one of the most important archaeological sites in Greece. Once a major religious and commercial center in antiquity, Delos is now an open-air museum and a UNESCO World Heritage Site. Visitors can take a ferry from Mykonos to Delos, where they can walk among the ruins of temples, houses, and marketplaces that date back to the 5th century BCE. The island is especially famous for its Sanctuary of Apollo and the Terrace of the Lions, where marble statues of lions, once guardians of the sacred area, now stand in majestic silence.

The Delos Archaeological Museum, open daily from 9:00 AM to 3:00 PM (closed on Mondays), houses a collection of artifacts from the site, providing valuable context for the ruins. Admission costs around €12 for adults.

Santorini is another island rich in cultural heritage, with the ruins of the ancient city of Akrotiri standing out as a prime attraction. This ancient Minoan city was buried in volcanic ash during a catastrophic eruption around 1600 BCE, preserving its buildings, frescoes, and everyday objects for thousands of years. Today, visitors can explore the remarkably well-preserved ruins, which offer a fascinating glimpse into the life of the ancient inhabitants. Akrotiri is often compared to Pompeii due to the way the volcanic eruption preserved the city. The site is open daily from 8:00 AM to 8:00 PM, and the entrance fee is approximately €12. The adjacent Akrotiri Museum in Fira, open from 8:00 AM to 8:00 PM, displays the artifacts discovered on the site, such as pottery, tools, and beautiful frescoes. These treasures offer insights into the artistic and everyday life of the people who once lived on the island.

Another significant historical site in Santorini is the Archaeological Museum of Thira, located in the island's capital, Fira. This museum showcases the island's history from the prehistoric to the classical period, with highlights including pottery, sculptures, and jewelry from the ancient city of Thira. The museum is open daily from 8:30 AM to 3:00 PM, and the entrance fee is typically around €6. The museum provides visitors with a comprehensive understanding of the island's past, from its ancient roots to its place in Greek history.

In addition to its archaeological sites, Santorini also boasts a rich tradition of art and crafts, much of which is still evident today. The island's artisans continue to produce beautiful works, from pottery to woven textiles, inspired by the island's natural surroundings and historical influences. Visitors to Santorini can explore local workshops, where they can purchase handcrafted goods or even observe the artisans at work. The island is particularly famous for its traditional pottery, which dates back to ancient times, and many studios in the villages of Pyrgos and Megalochori offer demonstrations and classes in pottery-making.

Mykonos, widely known for its vibrant nightlife, also has a rich cultural heritage that is reflected in its museums, traditional architecture, and local customs. The Mykonos Archaeological Museum, located in the town of Mykonos, houses a large collection of artifacts from the island's past, including sculptures, ceramics, and jewelry from the ancient period. One of the highlights of the museum is the collection of ancient Greek sculptures, including those of Apollo and Artemis, which offer insight into the island's significance as a religious and cultural center in antiquity. The museum is open daily from 9:00 AM to 3:00 PM, with an entry fee of approximately €6.

The town of Mykonos itself is a cultural treasure trove. Its narrow, winding streets, lined with whitewashed houses and colorful bougainvillea, preserve the island's traditional charm. The windmills of Mykonos, iconic symbols of the island, stand as reminders of the island's agricultural past. Once used to grind grain, these windmills now stand empty, offering visitors a picturesque backdrop for photos. Another cultural highlight of Mykonos is the Panagia Paraportiani Church, located in Mykonos Town. This striking white church, built in the 16th century, features a unique blend of architectural styles and is one of the most photographed landmarks in the Cyclades.

The island of Naxos, the largest of the Cyclades, is also home to a wealth of cultural heritage. The island's old town, Chora, offers a glimpse into traditional Greek life with its winding alleys and beautiful Venetian architecture. One of the most notable landmarks in Naxos is the Temple of Apollo, also known as the Portara. This massive marble doorway, the only remaining part of an unfinished temple, stands as a symbol of the island's ancient history. The Portara offers incredible views of the island's coastline, making it one of the most photographed sites in the Cyclades. The temple dates back to the 6th century BCE and is a testament to the island's important role in ancient Greek civilization.

Naxos is also home to several important museums, including the Archaeological Museum of Naxos, located in the heart of Chora. The museum displays artifacts from the island's ancient history, including sculptures, pottery, and inscriptions, many of which were discovered during excavations on the island. The museum is open daily from 8:30 AM to 3:00 PM, and the entrance fee is around €3. Visitors can learn about the island's rich past, from its ancient Greek heritage to its later Venetian and Ottoman influences.

While Naxos and Mykonos offer a rich historical experience, other islands in the Cyclades provide unique cultural experiences as well. The island of Paros, for example, is home to the charming town of Naoussa, a former fishing village that has retained its traditional character. Paros is also known for its marble, which has been used since antiquity in the construction of monuments and sculptures. The island's Archaeological Museum in Parikia showcases a variety of ancient artifacts, including sculptures, pottery, and tools, many of which were crafted from Parian marble.

The Cyclades are also known for their vibrant festivals and traditions, many of which have been celebrated for centuries. On the island of Tinos, the Feast of the Assumption, held on August 15th, is one of the most important religious festivals in Greece. Pilgrims from across the country travel to Tinos to visit the Panagia Evangelistria Church, which houses the miraculous icon of the Virgin Mary. The festival is a time of celebration, with processions, music, and traditional dances that bring the island's rich cultural heritage to life.

Suggested Itineraries

The Cyclades offer endless possibilities for exploration, each island boasting its own unique character and charm. Whether you're here for history, nature, or simply soaking in the sun, there's a perfect itinerary for every traveler. Here's a detailed guide to help you plan your journey through this beautiful group of islands, with routes designed to cover the highlights of the region while leaving room for personal discovery.

For those with a week to spare, a mix of the most iconic islands and some quieter, off-the-beaten-path destinations will provide a balanced experience. Start in Mykonos, where the glamour and energy of the island's nightlife contrast with its historical charm. Mykonos Town, with its maze of whitewashed streets and the picturesque windmills near the port, sets the stage for an unforgettable stay. Take some time to explore the Archaeological Museum of Mykonos to get a sense of the island's ancient significance. You can also visit the nearby Panagia Paraportiani Church, an iconic white church with a distinct architectural style that combines Byzantine, Gothic, and Venetian influences. Expect to spend at least half a day exploring Mykonos Town. It's free to wander, but museum entry is around €6, and the church is open all day for visitors.

From Mykonos, catch a ferry to Delos, a short 30-minute ride away. This small island is one of the most important archaeological sites in Greece and a UNESCO World Heritage site. The ruins of Delos date back to ancient times and are associated with the Greek gods Apollo and Artemis. The island is open daily from 9:00 AM to 3:00 PM, with a ticket price of €12. You can spend a few hours exploring the ruins, particularly the Temple of Apollo and the Terrace of the Lions. Be sure to take in the panoramic views from the top of the island, as it provides a great vantage point over the Aegean.

After Delos, take another short ferry ride to Paros, an island that balances historical charm and natural beauty. Paros' main town, Parikia, is home to the impressive Church of Panagia

Ekatontapiliani, one of the oldest and most important Christian monuments in Greece. Dating back to the 4th century, this church offers a glimpse into the island's long history. It's open daily, and visiting is free, though donations are welcome. In the afternoon, head to Naoussa, a picturesque village with narrow streets, seafood restaurants, and beautiful beaches. Spend the evening here, perhaps enjoying a meal by the sea.

A full day in Paros should also include a visit to the ancient marble quarries, where the famous Parian marble was once mined. This marble, which has been used in sculptures and monuments throughout history, is still prized for its quality. The quarries are located just outside the village of Marathi and can be accessed with a short hike. This area is relatively quiet, allowing visitors to explore at their own pace without the typical crowds.

From Paros, catch a ferry to Naxos, the largest island in the Cyclades. Naxos is an excellent place for those who love outdoor activities, particularly hiking. Spend a day exploring the island's inland villages, such as Halki and Filoti, where you'll find traditional whitewashed houses, charming narrow streets, and local tavernas offering delicious regional specialties like local cheeses and olives. If you're up for a challenge, hike up Mount Zeus, Naxos' highest peak, at 1,004 meters. The hike takes around 3-4 hours, but the breathtaking views of the island and surrounding islands make it worthwhile. Entrance is free, and the trails are well-marked.

After your hike, unwind at one of Naxos' many beaches, such as Agios Georgios, located near Naxos Town. This sandy beach is perfect for an afternoon swim or a relaxing sunbathe. It's easily accessible from the town, and you'll find plenty of beachfront cafes to enjoy a coffee or lunch.

From Naxos, take a ferry to the quieter island of Folegandros. This is a hidden gem within the Cyclades, offering a calm atmosphere and some of the most dramatic landscapes in the region. The island's main village, Chora, sits on a cliff offering sweeping views of the Aegean. A visit to the Church of Panagia, perched at the edge of the cliff, is a must. The church is open daily, and the hike to the top is an experience in itself, offering spectacular views of the coastline and the nearby islands.

Spend the next day exploring the island's beaches, such as Katergo Beach, which is only accessible by boat or via a steep hiking path. Its remote location means it's less crowded, providing an excellent spot for relaxation. Folegandros is ideal for anyone looking to escape the crowds, offering a more laid-back pace of life.

If you have an additional day or two, head to Ios, known for its lively nightlife, but also home to some charming, quiet spots. Ios is famous for its stunning beaches, and Manganari Beach stands out as one of the best on the island. It's a perfect spot to relax, swim, or enjoy water sports. You can also visit the tomb of the ancient Greek poet Homer, believed to be located near the island's main town, Chora. The tomb is situated at the top of a hill, offering great views of the surrounding area. The site is free to visit, but it's a bit of a hike, so bring comfortable shoes.

Finally, a short ferry ride from Ios will bring you to Santorini, the most famous of the Cyclades islands. Known for its breathtaking sunsets, whitewashed buildings, and volcanic landscapes, Santorini offers a variety of activities to suit any traveler. Spend your first day exploring Fira and Oia, the two most famous towns on the island. Both towns offer stunning views of the caldera, and wandering the narrow streets will lead you to cafes, shops, and art galleries. Visit the Museum of Prehistoric Thira to learn about the island's ancient history, including the eruption that destroyed the ancient Minoan city of Akrotiri. The museum is open daily from 8:00 AM to 8:00 PM, with a ticket price of €6.

One of the highlights of Santorini is the caldera itself, which can be explored on foot or by boat. A boat tour around the caldera offers views of the volcanic islands, and many tours include stops for swimming in the hot springs. Prices for boat tours vary, but expect to pay around €30-€50 per person for a half-day trip. For a more relaxed experience, head to one of Santorini's famous beaches, such as Kamari or Red Beach, to enjoy the crystal-clear waters and striking scenery.

After a day of sightseeing and relaxation, end your time on Santorini with a sunset at Oia, one of the most iconic spots in the world. Watching the sun dip below the horizon, casting an orange glow over the whitewashed buildings and the caldera, is an unforgettable experience.

For travelers with more time, a two-week itinerary through the Cyclades would allow for more in-depth exploration. You could spend a few extra days on each island, hiking, visiting smaller villages, or relaxing at quieter beaches. A two-week trip would also allow you to venture to some of the more remote islands, such as Sifnos or Kimolos, both of which offer a slower pace of life and incredible natural beauty.

Trip Planning

Getting there and around the Island

Reaching the Cyclades is straightforward, with a variety of options for getting to the islands from mainland Greece or other parts of the country. Once you're in the Cyclades, getting around is equally simple, with a mix of ferries, buses, taxis, and rental services available to help you explore the islands at your own pace.

Most travelers begin their journey to the Cyclades by flying into Athens, the most common point of entry for visitors heading to these islands. From Athens, you can catch a ferry to your desired island. Ferries to the Cyclades are frequent, especially during the summer months, and depart from the Port of Piraeus, which is easily accessible from central Athens. The ferry ride to most of the islands in the Cyclades typically takes between 1.5 to 4 hours, depending on your destination and the ferry type. High-speed ferries are quicker but tend to be more expensive, while regular ferries are a bit slower but offer a more relaxed ride. The cost of a ferry ticket can vary, ranging from €20 to €50 for a one-way trip, depending on the island you're traveling to and the type of ferry you choose. For example, a ferry from Piraeus to

Mykonos typically costs around €40, while a ferry to Naxos may be a bit cheaper at around €30. Ferries usually depart throughout the day, with more frequent services during the peak summer season.

Once in the Cyclades, you'll find that getting around the islands is a breeze. On many of the larger islands, such as Mykonos, Santorini, and Naxos, there is a robust network of local buses that make it easy to explore the island's attractions. The bus system on Mykonos, for example, is efficient and affordable, with buses running from the town of Mykonos to popular beaches like Paradise Beach and Platis Gialos. Buses on Mykonos typically run every 30 minutes to an hour, with a ticket price of around €2 per ride. The bus station in Mykonos Town is located near the old port, and buses depart regularly throughout the day until late evening. Santorini also has a good bus system, with regular services between the island's main towns, Fira and Oia, and popular beaches like Kamari and Perissa. Tickets generally cost around €1.80-€2.50, depending on the route, and buses run at regular intervals throughout the day, with some services extending into the evening.

For those who prefer a bit more flexibility, taxis are readily available on the islands, though they tend to be more expensive than buses. On Mykonos, for instance, a taxi ride from Mykonos Town to the airport costs around €20, while a short ride within the town can cost approximately €10. Taxis on the island are metered, but during peak tourist season, fares can be higher due to demand. On Santorini, taxis are available at the airport and the main bus station in Fira, with fares typically starting at €5 for a short trip and rising depending on the distance. One downside of taxis is that they can be difficult to find during busy times, particularly during the high season when demand often outstrips supply.

If you want to explore the islands at your own pace, renting a car, scooter, or ATV is an excellent option. Most of the larger islands in the Cyclades offer a wide range of rental services, and it's easy to find a rental office upon arrival. Renting a car can be a great way to explore the more remote parts of the islands, as it provides greater flexibility to visit smaller villages, secluded beaches, and archaeological sites. The cost of renting a car in the Cyclades usually starts at around €30-€40 per day for a small economy car, depending on the island and the season. Santorini and Mykonos, being more touristy, tend to have slightly higher rental rates, while islands like Naxos and Paros offer more affordable options. Scooters and ATVs are a popular alternative to cars, particularly on smaller islands, where the roads are narrow and less busy. Renting a scooter or ATV typically costs around €15-€25 per day, and rental agencies are common near the ports and main tourist areas.

On some islands, especially those with more rugged terrain like Naxos and Paros, you can also rent an off-road vehicle, which allows you to explore the island's hidden gems, including remote beaches and hiking trails. These vehicles are perfect for those who want to experience the islands' natural beauty away from the crowds. Rental companies on these islands can also provide recommendations on the best routes and destinations to visit, helping you make the most of your time on the island.

For those who want to enjoy the stunning Aegean waters, boat rentals are another popular option in the Cyclades. Renting a boat gives you the chance to explore the coastline and nearby islands, especially for those who want to visit isolated beaches that are only accessible by sea. On islands like Mykonos and Paros, boat rentals range from €100-€300 per day, depending on the size and type of the boat. You can rent a small motorboat without a license or hire a private yacht with a skipper for a more luxurious experience. There are also boat tours available, which allow you to explore the surrounding islands in a group or privately. A typical half-day boat tour to nearby islands like Delos or the volcanic islands of Santorini costs around €30-€50 per person. Some tours include lunch and drinks, providing an all-inclusive experience.

In addition to ferries, buses, taxis, and rental vehicles, the islands of the Cyclades also offer various private transport options, such as guided tours and transfers. Many hotels offer shuttle services to and from the ferry ports or airports, making it easier for visitors to get to their accommodations. In Mykonos, you'll find plenty of luxury transfers available, especially if you're staying in high-end resorts. These services are usually more expensive but provide a more comfortable and hassle-free way to get around. On smaller islands like Folegandros, you can find local taxi boats that transport you between various points on the island, providing a unique way to experience the island's coast. The cost of these boats varies depending on the distance, but expect to pay around €5-€10 per person for a short trip.

If you're keen on exploring the islands on foot, there are plenty of scenic walking trails to enjoy. In places like Naxos and Paros, where the landscapes are varied and stunning, hiking is a popular way to see the islands. Trails lead you through charming villages, olive groves, and along the coastline, offering some of the best views of the islands. In Naxos, for example, the trail to Mount Zeus is a challenging but rewarding hike that takes you to the highest peak on the island, providing sweeping views of the surrounding Aegean Sea and nearby islands. This hike is free and can take about 3-4 hours, depending on your pace.

When it comes to moving between islands, ferries are the primary mode of transport. The Cyclades have excellent ferry connections, and it's easy to hop between islands in a short amount of time. Ferries generally run from early morning until late afternoon, with some offering evening services during the summer months. However, ferry schedules can be subject to weather conditions, so it's always a good idea to check the timetable ahead of time and keep an eye on the weather. Most ferry companies also offer the option to purchase tickets in advance, either online or at the port. The larger islands like Mykonos, Santorini, and Naxos are well-connected, with ferries running frequently, while smaller islands might have fewer departures.

Accommodation Guide

The Cyclades offer a wide range of accommodation options that cater to every type of traveler, from luxury seekers to those looking for budget-friendly stays or something a little more off the beaten path. Whether you're planning to soak in the breathtaking views of Santorini, enjoy the lively atmosphere of Mykonos, or find solace on the quieter islands like Folegandros, there's no shortage of places to rest your head.

In Mykonos, the accommodation scene ranges from luxurious, five-star resorts with private pools and stunning sea views to cozy boutique hotels tucked away in narrow streets. Mykonos Town (Chora) is the island's hub, where most of the action happens. For those seeking ultimate luxury, resorts like the Myconian Ambassador Hotel & Thalasso Spa are worth considering. Located just a short distance from Platis Gialos Beach, this high-end hotel offers exceptional service, a spa, and a beautiful infinity pool overlooking the Aegean. Expect to pay around €300-€500 per night for a standard room, with prices rising significantly for suites and villas with private pools. The hotel is open year-round, though peak season sees the island bustling with visitors, so it's wise to book in advance.

For a more intimate experience, consider staying at a boutique hotel like the Bill & Coo Suites and Lounge. Situated a short distance from Mykonos Town, this adults-only hotel is known for its stunning views, sleek design, and personalized service. The rooms are spacious and modern, with many offering private balconies or pools. Prices typically range from €400 to €700 per night, with a variety of packages available for a tailored experience. It's a great choice for couples looking for a romantic getaway or those seeking a peaceful retreat from the lively streets of Mykonos Town.

If you're on a tighter budget, Mykonos also has plenty of affordable options. The Hotel Rochari, located near the heart of Mykonos Town, offers simple but comfortable rooms with traditional Cycladic architecture. Prices start at around €100-€150 per night for a double room, making it a more affordable choice without sacrificing the charm of staying in town. The hotel has a pool and is within walking distance to the famous windmills and Little Venice, making it a convenient base for exploring.

When it comes to Santorini, the range of accommodation reflects the island's reputation for romantic sunsets and high-end luxury. Oia, with its iconic blue-domed churches and cliffside views, is one of the most popular places to stay. For a truly memorable experience, consider booking a cave hotel, where rooms are carved into the cliffs, offering unbeatable views of the caldera. Hotels like Canaves Oia Suites & Spa offer a selection of suites that include plunge pools, incredible views, and easy access to the best sunset views. Prices here start at around €350 per night for a basic suite, but expect to pay upwards of €700 for a more luxurious option.

Fira, the capital of Santorini, offers a more vibrant, bustling atmosphere. For a central location with great views, stay at the Aressana Spa Hotel and Suites, located just a short walk from the town's bustling shops and restaurants. This hotel combines traditional Cycladic architecture with modern luxury, including a spa, pool, and spacious rooms. Prices here range from €250 to €400 per night, depending on the season. The hotel's location is perfect for those who want easy access to nightlife and shopping, as well as proximity to the island's famous viewpoints.

For those looking to save a bit more while still experiencing the beauty of Santorini, there are plenty of budget-friendly options, especially in Fira or Kamari. In Fira, try the Poppy's Studios, a simple but charming place with clean, comfortable rooms and a lovely garden. Prices start around €70-€100 per night, and while it may not have the same upscale amenities as the luxury hotels, it's a great base for exploring Santorini on a budget. Alternatively, in Kamari, a coastal town known for its black sand beach, the Hotel Arion offers affordable rooms with a pool and easy access to the beach for around €60-€90 per night.

Naxos is known for its laid-back vibe, and this is reflected in its accommodation options. While it does have its share of upscale resorts, many visitors come here for the more relaxed atmosphere, so you'll find plenty of charming guesthouses, small hotels, and family-run accommodations. In Naxos Town (Chora), the Hotel Grotta is a popular choice. It offers well-priced rooms with great views of the Aegean Sea and the ancient Temple of Apollo. Prices start at around €80 per night for a double room, and the hotel offers a peaceful location away from the busiest parts of the town, yet it's just a short walk to the main attractions and beach. The hotel is open year-round, making it a great option for those seeking a quieter stay during the off-season.

For a more intimate experience, head to the village of Apiranthos, nestled in the island's mountainous interior. The Katerina's Studios offers a charming, family-friendly option for those looking to escape the more tourist-heavy parts of Naxos. The studios are simple yet comfortable, and the quiet village offers a taste of traditional island life. Rooms start at about €50 per night, with stunning views of the surrounding hills and valleys.

Over on Paros, the island offers a mix of everything, from affordable options in Parikia to chic boutique stays in Naoussa. For something more exclusive, check out the Paros Agnanti Hotel, situated just outside Parikia, offering beautiful rooms with sea views, a pool, and a fantastic restaurant. Prices for a standard room start at around €150-€200 per night. It's a lovely spot for those looking to relax and enjoy some peace away from the busier areas.

For a more budget-friendly option in Parikia, consider staying at the Hotel Paros, located a short walk from the main port. Offering simple, clean rooms at affordable rates, starting at €60-€90 per night, this hotel is a good choice for travelers who prioritize location and comfort without the hefty price tag. It's a great base for exploring the island, especially with its proximity to the beach and the old town.

Folegandros, known for its dramatic landscapes and peaceful atmosphere, is the perfect destination for those looking to escape the crowds. The island's accommodations are mostly family-run guesthouses and boutique hotels. A great option for those seeking an authentic experience is the Anemomilos Hotel in Chora, which offers rooms with stunning sea views, located just a short walk from the main square. Prices here range from €100 to €150 per night. For a more secluded experience, try the Folegandros Apartments, located in a quieter area of the island with easy access to the island's hiking trails and beaches. Rooms start at around €80 per night, and the apartments are an excellent choice for those seeking a homey, relaxed atmosphere.

Sustainable Travel

Sustainable travel in the Cyclades is becoming increasingly important as tourism grows and the islands continue to attract travelers from around the world. The natural beauty, traditional architecture, and rich culture of the islands make them irresistible, but the increase in visitors has also led to concerns about environmental preservation and local well-being. Fortunately, a growing movement toward eco-conscious travel has emerged, allowing visitors to enjoy the Cyclades while minimizing their impact on the islands' fragile ecosystems and supporting local communities. Here's how you can travel sustainably while exploring the gems of the Cyclades.

One of the most significant aspects of sustainable travel in the Cyclades is transportation. Ferries remain the most common way to get between the islands, and many ferry companies have made efforts to become more environmentally friendly by adopting newer, more fuel-efficient vessels. Blue Star

Ferries, one of the largest ferry operators in Greece, has introduced environmentally conscious initiatives such as reducing fuel consumption and implementing waste recycling onboard. Ferry tickets typically range from €20 to €50, depending on the distance and type of ferry. When booking your ferry, consider traveling with companies that prioritize eco-friendly practices and look for those that offer high-speed ferries with lower emissions.

Once on the islands, getting around with minimal environmental impact is also possible. Many of the Cycladic islands, such as Santorini, Mykonos, and Naxos, offer bike rentals, which is one of the most eco-friendly ways to explore the islands. Renting a bike not only reduces your carbon footprint but also provides an intimate experience of the islands, allowing you to access areas that might be missed when using motorized transport. In Mykonos, for example, companies like Mykonos Bike Rentals offer a range of bikes for about €15-€25 per day, allowing you to cycle around the island's quieter areas, far from the bustling town center. If you're visiting Naxos, the island's bike rental options are even more abundant, with rentals typically starting at €12-€20 per day. Naxos is particularly bike-friendly, with scenic paths that lead you through villages and to stunning beaches like Agios Georgios.

Scooter and electric vehicle rentals are also available on several islands, offering an alternative to traditional cars. Some companies, such as Green Scooters on Mykonos, focus on eco-friendly electric scooters, which allow you to zip around the island with minimal environmental impact. The prices for renting an electric scooter typically range from €20 to €30 per day, and they are a convenient, fun, and sustainable way to explore the islands without adding to traffic or emissions.

In addition to using eco-friendly transport options, sustainable travelers in the Cyclades can also embrace sustainable accommodations. Many hotels, hostels, and guesthouses are beginning to adopt green practices, focusing on energy efficiency, waste reduction, and supporting local products and businesses. In Santorini, the Astra Suites is a standout example of a sustainable luxury hotel. This five-star hotel has made strides to reduce its carbon footprint by using solar energy to heat water, employing energy-efficient systems, and supporting local agriculture by sourcing ingredients from nearby farms. Rooms here typically start around €350 per night, reflecting both its luxury offerings and commitment to sustainability. Smaller guesthouses like the EcoHouse in Mykonos also take pride in their sustainable practices, using locally sourced building materials and minimizing waste.

Rates here range from €80 to €150 per night, offering a more affordable option while still being eco-conscious.

Another crucial element of sustainable travel in the Cyclades is the use of local and organic food. The islands are blessed with a bounty of fresh produce, local cheeses, seafood, and wines that are integral to the region's culinary identity. Many restaurants are now focusing on serving local and seasonal ingredients, reducing food miles and supporting the island's agricultural traditions. In Mykonos, Kiki's Tavern, located near Agios Sostis Beach, is known for its farm-to-table approach, offering delicious, simple Greek dishes made from locally sourced produce. It's a popular spot that stays true to the island's agricultural roots, and meals typically cost around €15-€20 per person. Santorini, too, has embraced this trend, with places like Metaxi Mas, located on the outskirts of Pyrgos, serving meals made with ingredients sourced from the island's fertile soil. Dining here costs around €20-€35 per person, and the focus is on high-quality, locally grown produce.

Naxos is another island where local food plays a huge role in sustainability. The island is known for its agricultural heritage, particularly its cheese, potatoes, and olive oil. In the village of Halki, you'll find the Naxos Olive Oil Company, a family-run operation that produces some of the island's finest olive oil.

Visitors can tour the mill, learn about the production process, and sample the different oils, all while supporting a local business committed to sustainable farming. Tours typically cost around €10-€15 per person, and the olive oil is available for purchase. Similarly, Naxos' traditional market in Chora sells organic produce from the island's farms, making it easy to stock up on fresh, local ingredients for your stay.

Waste reduction is another essential component of sustainable travel in the Cyclades. While the islands are beautiful, they are also vulnerable to the waste created by tourism, especially plastic waste. Visitors are encouraged to bring reusable water bottles and avoid single-use plastics by purchasing products from local shops that offer eco-friendly packaging. Many shops now offer alternatives to plastic bags, encouraging shoppers to bring their own reusable bags. Additionally, several islands have waste disposal systems in place that separate recyclables from general waste, and businesses that use these systems are becoming more common.

If you're looking to experience the Cyclades in a sustainable way, consider participating in activities that help protect the environment. In the waters surrounding the islands, marine life is under pressure from tourism and fishing. Organizations such as the Aegean Rebreath in Santorini work to promote sustainable diving and marine conservation. The group organizes underwater clean-up initiatives, where volunteers help to remove plastic waste and other debris from the ocean floor. Participating in these activities is a great way to give back to the islands while also learning more about their delicate ecosystems. Diving trips in the region usually range from €50-€90 per person, with the added benefit of contributing to marine conservation efforts.

Hiking is another excellent way to explore the Cyclades sustainably. The islands' rugged landscapes are perfect for walking, and there are numerous hiking trails that allow you to enjoy the natural beauty without contributing to carbon emissions. Naxos, for example, has a number of well-marked hiking paths that take you through ancient olive groves, traditional villages, and up to the island's highest peak, Mount Zeus. These trails are free to explore, and you'll likely encounter few others along the way, giving you a sense of solitude and immersion in the island's natural environment.

Sustainable travel in the Cyclades extends beyond environmental consciousness; it's also about supporting local communities and respecting the cultural heritage of the islands. Visiting smaller, lesser-known islands like Serifos or Folegandros can provide you with a more authentic experience while helping to disperse tourism more evenly across the region. These quieter islands are more reliant on tourism to support their economies, but they offer an opportunity to travel more responsibly while immersing yourself in traditional island life.

Shopping Tips

Shopping in the Cyclades offers a delightful mix of high-quality local products, handcrafted goods, and unique souvenirs that will make your visit memorable. From artisan goods to traditional Greek items, the islands provide a variety of shopping experiences that reflect the culture and spirit of the Aegean. Whether you're wandering through bustling market streets in Mykonos or discovering hidden gems in Naxos, there's something for everyone looking to bring home a piece of the islands.

In Mykonos, shopping is a mix of luxury boutiques, high-end fashion stores, and local artisan shops. The main shopping areas are around Mykonos Town (Chora), where you'll find narrow streets lined with small shops selling everything from handmade jewelry and clothing to fine art and designer goods. The island is particularly known for its unique, hand-crafted jewelry. For exquisite, locally made pieces, head to places like Yannis, which is tucked in the heart of Mykonos Town. This jewelry shop offers intricate designs that incorporate elements of Greek mythology, often using silver, gold, and semi-precious stones. A piece of jewelry here can cost anywhere from €50 to several hundred euros, depending on the complexity and materials used. The shop is open daily from 10:00 AM to 9:00 PM during peak season.

For those seeking fashion, Mykonos doesn't disappoint. Boutiques such as "Funky Buddha" or "Kostantinos" offer stylish clothing with a modern twist on Greek fashion, with prices for a chic outfit starting around €100-€200. While these stores carry international brands, they also showcase unique designs that incorporate local craftsmanship, ideal for those wanting to take home something truly special.

If you're after authentic Greek souvenirs, Mykonos has several stores that focus on traditional crafts. Look for places that sell handmade leather goods, like bags, sandals, and wallets. A favorite among tourists is the shop "Leather by Asteria," located in the heart of Mykonos Town. Their handmade leather sandals, which start at around €30, come in a variety of styles, from minimalist to more elaborate designs. The store is open from 10:00 AM to 8:00 PM daily, and you can watch artisans create the sandals right in front of you, making it an educational shopping experience.

Moving on to Santorini, the island is known for its distinctive products, including local wines, volcanic stone jewelry, and traditional crafts. One of the highlights of Santorini shopping is the wine. Santorini is home to some of Greece's most famous vineyards, producing the renowned Assyrtiko wine. You can buy bottles directly from local wineries like Santo Wines, which has a lovely wine shop with a tasting area overlooking the caldera. Bottles of Assyrtiko range from €10 to €30, depending on the vintage. The shop is open daily from 10:00 AM to 7:00 PM, and it's the perfect place to pick up a bottle or two as a memento of your visit.

Another must-buy in Santorini is volcanic stone jewelry. The island's unique volcanic heritage makes it a great place to pick up jewelry made from these stones. You'll find shops specializing in this in Oia, such as "Art of the Stone," which features hand-crafted pieces using lava rock and silver. Prices for a necklace or bracelet range from €40 to €150, with some items featuring small gemstones set within the volcanic rock, adding a touch of sparkle to the rough-hewn stone.

For something uniquely local, head to the small shops selling handcrafted pottery. Santorini's pottery reflects its ancient artistic traditions, with vibrant designs and patterns that often incorporate motifs of the sea, the sun, and ancient Greek symbols. You can find these pieces in stores like "Diko's Art" in Fira, where you can buy small bowls, plates, and decorative items starting at €20. The shop is open from 9:00 AM to 8:00

PM and provides a wide range of pottery, perfect for anyone looking to take home a traditional piece of Greek craftsmanship.

In Naxos, shopping offers a more laid-back and authentic experience. The island is known for its high-quality food products, especially its cheese, olive oil, and potatoes. A visit to the Naxos Market in Chora is a must for food lovers, where you can sample local cheeses like Graviera, a nutty and sweet cheese, and buy bottles of locally produced olive oil. In Naxos, olive oil is taken very seriously, and many producers offer guided tours of their groves. Naxos Olive Oil Company is a popular choice, and you can purchase a 500ml bottle for around €8-€12. The shop is open daily from 9:00 AM to 6:00 PM, and they also offer a range of soaps and skincare products made from olive oil.

In addition to food products, Naxos is home to a number of artisan shops selling handwoven textiles and local crafts. The island's artisans continue to produce traditional woven goods, including blankets, tablecloths, and towels, all crafted by hand. A great place to pick up these items is "Naxos Weaving," located in the heart of Chora. Prices for handwoven products start at €25 for small items like napkins, and you can find larger items like blankets for €80-€120. The shop is open daily, from 10:00 AM to 7:00 PM, and offers a glimpse into the traditional craft that has been passed down through generations.

Paros, known for its charming villages and traditional Cycladic beauty, offers an excellent variety of shopping options as well. The island is famous for its marble, and visitors can find shops that sell beautifully crafted marble items, such as sculptures, vases, and decorative objects. The Parian Marble Workshop in Parikia is one of the best places to find high-quality marble pieces, with prices ranging from €30 for small items to €200 or more for larger sculptures. The workshop is open daily from 9:00 AM to 7:00 PM, and you can watch the artisans at work.

Paros also has a number of excellent local craft shops, selling hand-knitted shawls, scarves, and intricate jewelry. In the village of Naoussa, you'll find the shop "Margarita" which specializes in traditional Greek clothing made from natural fibers, perfect for those looking to buy something unique and authentic. Prices for these handmade garments start at around €50-€100. The shop is open from 10:00 AM to 9:00 PM.

.

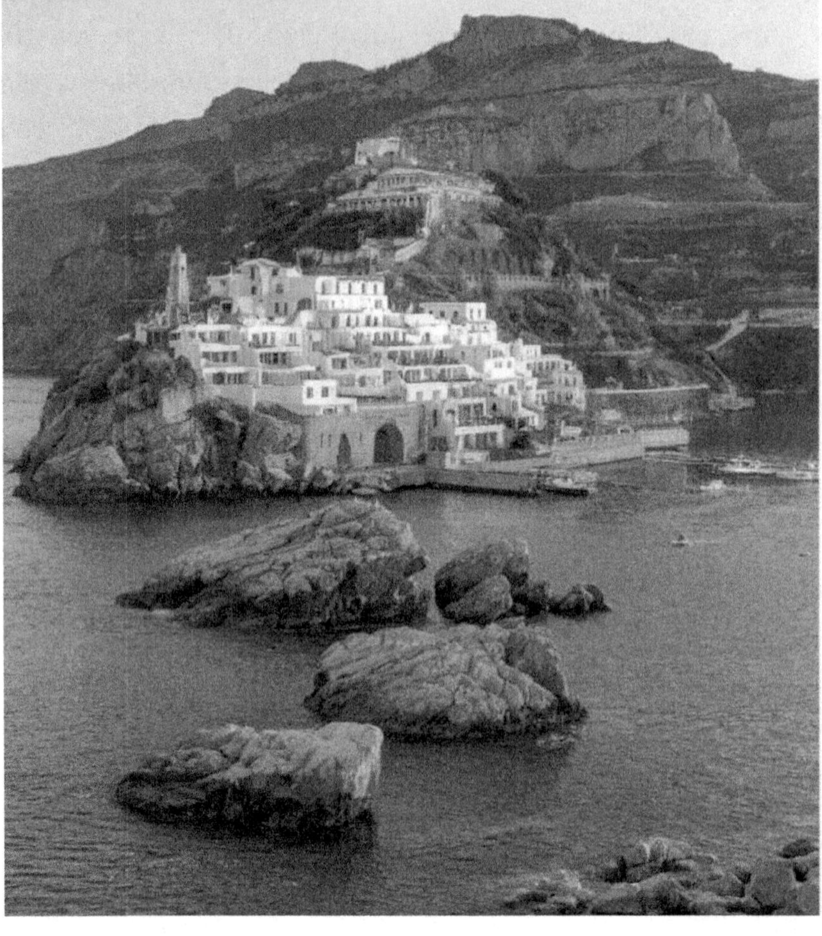

Must-Visit Islands

Santorini

Santorini, one of the most iconic destinations in the Cyclades, is known for its breathtaking beauty, stunning sunsets, and unique volcanic landscapes. Visitors flock to this island for its whitewashed buildings, blue-domed churches, crystal-clear waters, and fascinating history. From the bustling streets of Fira to the quieter corners of Oia, Santorini offers something for everyone—whether you're looking to relax by the beach, explore ancient ruins, or enjoy world-class dining with a view.

Santorini's caldera, formed by a massive volcanic eruption around 3,600 years ago, is its most striking feature. The steep cliffs of the caldera are home to some of the island's most famous villages, including Fira, Oia, and Imerovigli. These villages offer a combination of stunning views, charming streets, and a wealth of shops, restaurants, and accommodations. The island's picturesque streets, lined with white-washed houses, narrow alleys, and bougainvillea, make for a perfect spot to wander, explore, and take in the atmosphere.

Oia, perched on the northern tip of the island, is perhaps the most famous village on Santorini, especially for its unforgettable sunsets. Visitors from around the world flock to Oia's vantage points to catch the sun dipping below the horizon, casting a golden glow over the caldera and the Aegean Sea. The village itself is a maze of narrow lanes and steps, with charming cafes, art galleries, and boutiques offering local crafts and goods. If you're looking for something truly special, be sure to stop by the numerous jewelry shops, where you can find unique pieces made from gold, silver, and volcanic stones. Prices for jewelry typically start around €50 and can go up to several hundred euros, depending on the design.

Fira, the capital of Santorini, is a lively hub full of shops, restaurants, and bars. It's also home to several museums, including the Museum of Prehistoric Thira, which showcases artifacts from the ancient city of Akrotiri, as well as ancient pottery, sculptures, and frescoes. Akrotiri, an archaeological site located near the village of Akrotiri, is one of the most significant sites in Santorini. This ancient Minoan city was buried by volcanic ash in the 16th century BCE, and today, visitors can explore its well-preserved streets, homes, and frescoes. The site is open daily from 8:00 AM to 8:00 PM, with an entrance fee of €12. The nearby Akrotiri Archaeological Museum in Fira also provides valuable insight into the site's history and is open from 8:00 AM to 8:00 PM for €6.

For beach lovers, Santorini offers a variety of beaches, each with its own unique character. Kamari Beach, on the eastern side of the island, is one of the most popular, with its black sand created by the island's volcanic activity. Here, you'll find a variety of beach bars, restaurants, and water sports rentals. The beach is well-equipped with sunbeds, umbrellas, and facilities for visitors, making it a great spot for a relaxing day by the sea. Another popular beach is Perissa Beach, also known for its black sand, where the coastline stretches for several kilometers. Both beaches are free to access, though renting a sunbed usually costs around €10-€20 for the day.

For a more secluded experience, head to the Red Beach, located near Akrotiri. The striking red cliffs and the calm waters make this beach a popular spot, though it can get crowded during peak season. To reach the beach, you'll need to hike down a rocky path, but the stunning scenery makes the effort worthwhile. The beach is free to access, though it's best to go early in the morning to avoid the crowds.

Santorini is also known for its exceptional dining options, many of which offer stunning views of the caldera. One of the best places to enjoy the island's culinary offerings is in Oia, where you'll find restaurants with terraces overlooking the sea. For a fine dining experience, try "Astra Suites" in Oia, where you can enjoy Mediterranean-inspired cuisine with a panoramic view of the caldera. The prices here are on the higher end, with main courses starting around €25, but the experience and the view make it well worth the cost. Another great option in Oia is "Karma", offering a more relaxed atmosphere and delicious Greek dishes like moussaka and grilled seafood. Expect to pay around €20-€40 for a meal, depending on the dishes you choose.

Wine lovers will also appreciate Santorini's wine scene, as the island is famous for its Assyrtiko grape. The volcanic soil provides the perfect conditions for producing unique wines with a crisp and mineral taste. Several wineries on the island offer tours and tastings, where you can sample some of the best local wines while enjoying views of the vineyards and caldera. Santo Wines, located near Pyrgos, is one of the most popular wineries on the island. It offers daily wine tastings and tours, with prices starting at €20 per person for a tasting of four wines. The winery is open daily from 10:00 AM to 7:00 PM and provides stunning views of the caldera while you sip your wine.

Santorini is also home to several charming villages where you can experience a more authentic side of island life. Pyrgos, a quiet village located in the center of the island, offers narrow streets, whitewashed houses, and panoramic views. The village's main attraction is the medieval Pyrgos Castle, which offers incredible views over the entire island. The village is less touristy than Oia and Fira, making it a great place to escape the crowds and enjoy a peaceful stroll through traditional streets.

For those looking to experience Santorini's natural beauty, a hike to the top of the island's highest peak, Mount Profitis Ilias, is a must. The hike takes around 1.5 hours from the village of Pyrgos, and the summit offers panoramic views of the island and the surrounding Aegean Sea. It's a great way to see the island from a different perspective, away from the usual tourist spots. The mountain is home to a monastery that dates back to the 18th century and is open to visitors. The hike is free to access, though it's best to wear sturdy shoes and bring plenty of water.

Santorini is also an excellent destination for those seeking unique shopping experiences. The island is known for its high-quality local goods, such as handmade jewelry, pottery, and textiles. Shops in Oia, Fira, and Pyrgos offer beautiful pieces of jewelry crafted from silver and gold, often featuring designs inspired by the island's history and mythology. The prices can range from €30 for simple pieces to several hundred euros for more intricate designs. For pottery, head to the "Santorini Arts Factory" in Vlychada, which showcases local ceramic art. You can purchase handmade pottery, including vases, plates, and bowls, with prices ranging from €20 to €100.

Mykonos

Mykonos, one of the most famous islands in the Cyclades, is a vibrant mix of cosmopolitan energy, traditional Greek charm, and stunning coastal beauty. Known for its lively nightlife, picturesque streets, and crystal-clear waters, Mykonos attracts visitors from around the globe, offering a diverse range of experiences. Whether you're here to party, relax by the beach, or explore the island's historical sites, Mykonos has something to offer.

The heart of Mykonos is Mykonos Town (Chora), a charming maze of narrow streets lined with whitewashed houses, blue shutters, and vibrant bougainvillea. The town is a delightful place to get lost, with its boutique shops, art galleries, and cafes offering a true taste of island life. While the daytime is relatively peaceful, the streets come alive in the evening, with locals and visitors alike flocking to the bustling restaurants and bars. You'll find high-end fashion boutiques and art galleries alongside local shops selling handcrafted jewelry, ceramics, and leather goods. Wander through the picturesque alleys, stopping by iconic spots like the Windmills of Mykonos, which stand tall on a hill near the town. These traditional windmills are one of the most photographed spots on the island and offer sweeping views of the surrounding area.

Mykonos Town also boasts some of the island's best nightlife. The area around the Old Port is home to numerous bars, clubs, and restaurants, many of which stay open late into the night. The town's nightlife scene is a significant draw for party-goers, with world-renowned clubs like Cavo Paradiso and Skandinavian Bar offering international DJs and an electric atmosphere. However, even if you're not into the party scene, Mykonos Town has its quieter moments, with cozy tavernas where you can enjoy a meal with a view. Dining here ranges from casual street food to upscale Mediterranean restaurants, where you can try fresh seafood dishes like grilled octopus or moussaka, priced at around €15-€30 per person.

While Mykonos is well-known for its nightlife, it also offers several quiet and scenic spots perfect for those seeking a more laid-back experience. For beach lovers, Mykonos is home to some of the most beautiful beaches in Greece, many of which are just a short drive from the town. The famous Paradise Beach, located on the southern coast of the island, is a hotspot for sunbathers and party-goers alike. It offers beach clubs and bars, with sunbeds available for rent at around €10-€20. If you're looking for a quieter alternative, consider visiting Agios Sostis Beach. Tucked away on the northern side of the island, Agios Sostis remains less commercialized and offers a peaceful setting perfect for swimming and relaxing. It's free to access, but you'll want to bring your own beach essentials as there are no beach bars or facilities here.

Another hidden gem is Elia Beach, which is known for its clear waters and family-friendly atmosphere. It's more secluded than Paradise Beach but still offers plenty of amenities, including sunbeds, umbrellas, and water sports. The beach is free to access, but renting a sunbed typically costs around €15-€25 per day. The island is also known for its charming smaller beaches, such as Fokos Beach and Panormos Beach, which offer tranquility and natural beauty. Many of these beaches are surrounded by rocky landscapes and are perfect for those looking to escape the crowds.

In addition to its natural beauty, Mykonos is steeped in history and culture. A visit to the Archaeological Museum of Mykonos offers a glimpse into the island's ancient past, with artifacts from the nearby island of Delos, a UNESCO World Heritage site. Delos, located just 30 minutes by ferry from Mykonos, is one of Greece's most important archaeological sites. The island was once a major religious and commercial center and is home to the ruins of temples, marketplaces, and statues dating back to the 5th century BCE. The museum is open daily from 9:00 AM to 3:00 PM, with an entry fee of approximately €6. A day trip to Delos is highly recommended, as the island's archaeological sites are beautifully preserved, and the views over the Aegean Sea are unforgettable.

For those interested in traditional Mykonian culture, a visit to the Mykonos Folklore Museum is a must. Housed in a 19th-century mansion, the museum offers a fascinating look at the island's history, with exhibits ranging from traditional costumes and household items to maritime artifacts. The museum is open from 10:00 AM to 1:00 PM and 6:00 PM to 9:00 PM daily, with an entrance fee of around €3. It's a great way to learn more about the island's past and see how life has evolved over the centuries.

Mykonos is also famous for its windmills, which are scattered across the island, but the most iconic ones are located just above Mykonos Town. These windmills were originally used to grind grain and have become a symbol of the island. One of the most famous windmills, the "Kato Mili" windmill, stands near the Old Port, and is free to visit. The windmills offer panoramic views of the town and the sea, and it's a popular spot for sunset viewing.

If you're looking for a bit of adventure, consider exploring Mykonos by bike or scooter. Renting a scooter or ATV is a popular way to navigate the island, especially if you want to visit more remote beaches or explore the countryside. Rental prices for a scooter typically range from €15 to €30 per day, while ATVs can be rented for €30-€50 per day. Renting a car is also an option, but due to the narrow, winding streets of Mykonos Town, many people prefer scooters for their flexibility and ease of use.

For a more serene experience, explore the island's traditional villages, where you can experience local life and shop for unique handcrafted goods. The village of Ano Mera, located in the center of the island, is a charming, less-visited area with traditional whitewashed houses, quiet streets, and a lovely central square. The Panagia Tourliani Monastery, located in the heart of the village, is worth a visit, with its impressive architecture and peaceful atmosphere. The monastery is open daily from 9:00 AM to 1:00 PM and 5:00 PM to 8:00 PM, and entrance is free.

In terms of shopping, Mykonos offers a wide range of options, from high-end designer boutiques to local artisan shops. The streets of Mykonos Town are lined with chic shops selling everything from fashionable clothing and accessories to jewelry and artwork. Local markets and small shops also offer traditional goods, such as handmade leather sandals, woven textiles, and Greek ceramics. Prices for these souvenirs typically range from €10 for smaller items to €50 or more for higher-quality products. The island is especially known for its jewelry, with many local shops offering intricate designs inspired by Greek mythology, using silver, gold, and semi-precious stones.

Naxos

Naxos, the largest and greenest island in the Cyclades, offers a rich blend of ancient history, traditional villages, and stunning landscapes. With its rugged mountains, fertile valleys, and long stretches of beautiful beaches, Naxos has managed to retain a sense of authenticity and calm despite its growing popularity. This island is perfect for those who want to experience the true heart of Greece, combining cultural exploration, outdoor activities, and time spent relaxing on idyllic shores.

Naxos Town (Chora), the island's capital, serves as the hub for all activities and is a perfect starting point for any visit. The town is a maze of whitewashed houses and narrow alleys, with its historic center offering a combination of Byzantine, Venetian, and Greek architectural influences. The first thing you'll notice as you approach Chora is the impressive Portara, a massive marble doorway that stands at the entrance to the island's ancient Temple of Apollo. The temple, dating back to the 6th century BCE, was never completed, but the Portara remains a stunning symbol of Naxos. You can visit the Portara at any time, and it's especially popular at sunset, when the views over the sea and the surrounding area are nothing short of spectacular.

Wandering through Chora's winding streets, you'll encounter charming shops selling local products, including Naxos' famous cheeses, olives, and pottery. The island is renowned for its cheese, particularly its graviera, a nutty, hard cheese that pairs beautifully with local wines. Several small markets in Chora, including the one near the main square, offer these products for sale, allowing you to sample them as you shop. You'll also find handmade pottery in traditional shops, perfect for those looking to take home a piece of the island's craftsmanship. A small ceramic plate or bowl from Naxos typically costs around €20-€30, while larger, more intricate pieces can go for upwards of €50.

For those interested in the island's ancient history, the Archaeological Museum of Naxos, located in Chora, provides a fascinating insight into the island's past. The museum is housed in a neoclassical building and showcases a rich collection of ancient artifacts, including pottery, sculptures, and inscriptions. Entry costs around €3, and the museum is open daily from 8:30 AM to 3:00 PM, making it a great stop to learn about Naxos' role in ancient Greek civilization. One of the highlights of the museum is the collection of statues from the ancient temple of Demeter, which give visitors a deeper understanding of the island's religious practices and artistic heritage.

Not far from the town center lies the Kastro, a Venetian castle built in the 13th century. The castle, which sits on a hill above the town, offers sweeping views of Naxos Town and the surrounding area. As you explore the castle's narrow streets and discover hidden corners, you'll feel as though you've stepped back in time. The Kastro is free to visit and open daily, though it's best to visit during the daytime for optimal views and exploration.

While Naxos Town offers a wealth of historical and cultural attractions, the island's true charm lies in its countryside. The fertile valleys and rolling hills of Naxos are dotted with traditional villages that have remained largely unchanged for centuries. A visit to the village of Apiranthos, located in the island's mountainous interior, offers a glimpse into traditional island life. Apiranthos is known for its marble-paved streets, whitewashed houses, and picturesque surroundings. The village is home to several small museums, including the Folklore Museum, which showcases traditional artifacts, tools, and textiles. The museum is open from 10:00 AM to 1:00 PM and 5:00 PM to 8:00 PM, and entry costs around €2.

Another charming village worth visiting is Halki, situated in the island's heart. This village is famous for its local distillery, which produces the island's famous citron liqueur, a refreshing drink made from the citron fruit. The Vallindras Distillery offers free tours where you can learn about the production process and sample the liqueur. A bottle of citron liqueur from the distillery typically costs around €15-€20, making it a perfect souvenir to bring home.

For those who enjoy hiking, Naxos offers some of the best trails in the Cyclades. The island's mountainous terrain is perfect for outdoor enthusiasts looking to explore its natural beauty. One of the most popular hikes is to Mount Zeus, the highest peak on the island, which rises to 1,004 meters. The hike to the summit takes about 3-4 hours and offers stunning panoramic views of Naxos and the surrounding islands. Along the way, you'll pass through ancient olive groves, traditional villages, and dramatic landscapes. It's a challenging but rewarding hike, with a breathtaking payoff at the top. The hike is free to access, and the trailhead is located near the village of Filoti.

For beach lovers, Naxos offers a variety of beaches, from long stretches of sand to quieter coves. Agios Georgios Beach, located just a short walk from Naxos Town, is one of the most popular beaches on the island, known for its calm waters and sandy shoreline. It's a great spot for swimming, sunbathing, and water sports, with plenty of cafes and restaurants along the beach. Sunbeds and umbrellas can be rented for around €10-€15 per day, and the beach is well-equipped with facilities such as showers and changing rooms.

If you prefer a more secluded experience, head to Mikri Vigla Beach on the island's southwestern coast. This beach is less crowded than Agios Georgios and is perfect for those looking for a peaceful place to relax. The beach is also a popular spot for windsurfing and kitesurfing, with several water sports schools offering rentals and lessons. Mikri Vigla is free to access, though there are no facilities, so it's best to bring your own snacks and drinks.

Naxos is also home to some of the best beach bars in the Cyclades, where you can enjoy a drink while watching the sunset. The beach bar at Agia Anna Beach, a quieter beach located just south of Agios Georgios, is a great place to unwind after a day in the sun. The bar serves fresh fruit juices, cocktails, and light snacks, with prices for drinks starting at around €5-€10.

For food lovers, Naxos offers a wide range of culinary delights, with a strong emphasis on locally grown ingredients. Naxos is known for its excellent cheeses, including the famous graviera, as well as its potatoes and olives. Traditional tavernas across the island serve dishes made from fresh, local produce, with popular options including lamb kleftiko (slow-cooked lamb), moussaka, and fresh seafood. A typical meal at a taverna will cost around €15-€25 per person, depending on the restaurant and the dishes you order. In Chora, a great place to enjoy local cuisine is the "To Elliniko" taverna, which serves traditional Greek dishes in a cozy, welcoming atmosphere.

Naxos is also a great destination for those looking to shop for local products. The island's markets and shops sell a variety of handmade goods, including pottery, textiles, and jewelry. Naxos Weaving, a traditional textile workshop in Chora, offers handwoven scarves, blankets, and towels, with prices ranging from €20 to €100. You can also find locally made leather sandals and bags in small shops throughout the town, with prices starting at around €30-€40.

Paros

Paros, a jewel of the Cyclades, is an island that combines stunning landscapes, rich history, and a laid-back atmosphere, offering a perfect blend of everything the Greek islands have to offer. Whether you're drawn to its quaint villages, gorgeous beaches, or ancient ruins, Paros has an undeniable charm that leaves a lasting impression on anyone who visits.

The heart of Paros is Parikia, the island's main town, where traditional Greek architecture meets a lively atmosphere. The town is a maze of narrow streets filled with whitewashed houses, colorful bougainvillea, and bustling shops. As you wander through Parikia, one of the first sights you'll encounter is the Church of Panagia Ekatontapiliani, a remarkable Byzantine church that dates back to the 4th century. The church is one of the oldest and most significant religious sites in Greece, known for its stunning architecture and peaceful atmosphere. The church is open daily from 8:00 AM to 7:00 PM, and entry is free, although donations are appreciated. Inside, you'll find intricate mosaics and beautiful frescoes that showcase the island's rich religious history.

Just a short walk from the church, you'll find the Archaeological Museum of Paros, which provides a fascinating glimpse into the island's ancient past. The museum features a collection of sculptures, pottery, and artifacts from the island's long history, including pieces from the nearby ancient site of Delos. One of the most important exhibits is the statue of the "Parian Marble," which was once used to make ancient sculptures. The museum is open daily from 8:30 AM to 3:00 PM, with an entrance fee of around €3, making it a great stop for history enthusiasts looking to learn more about Paros' rich cultural heritage.

As you explore Parikia, take time to visit the Venetian Castle, which stands proudly over the town. Built in the 13th century by the Venetians, the castle is a fascinating historical site and offers panoramic views of the town and surrounding areas. The castle is free to visit and is open from 9:00 AM to 6:00 PM. It's a great spot to escape the crowds and enjoy some quiet moments while soaking in the view. The castle's remnants, including its walls and the medieval structures, make it a must-see for anyone interested in Paros' history.

For those who want to experience more of Paros' traditional charm, head to the village of Naoussa, located on the northern side of the island. Naoussa is one of the most picturesque villages in the Cyclades, with its charming harbor, narrow streets, and whitewashed houses. The village is known for its vibrant atmosphere, especially in the evening when the restaurants and bars along the harbor come alive. Naoussa's harbor is home to a number of fishing boats, and you'll often see local fishermen unloading their catch of the day. The waterfront is dotted with cafes and tavernas where you can enjoy a meal while watching the boats come in. Dining here usually costs around €15-€30 per person, depending on the restaurant and dishes you choose.

While Naoussa is famous for its nightlife and dining scene, it's also a great place to explore during the day. Strolling through its cobbled streets, you'll discover a number of boutique shops selling handmade goods, local art, and jewelry. The village is also home to the Naoussa Maritime Museum, which offers insights into the island's long maritime history. The museum is open from 9:00 AM to 2:00 PM and 6:00 PM to 9:00 PM, with an entrance fee of €3. Here, you can learn about Paros' role in ancient seafaring and its connection to other islands in the Aegean.

For a change of pace, Paros offers some of the best beaches in the Cyclades. One of the most famous is Kolymbithres Beach, located in the northern part of the island near Naoussa. This beach is known for its striking rock formations, with smooth, sculpted granite rocks creating natural pools where visitors can swim. Kolymbithres is a relatively quiet beach, ideal for those looking for a peaceful spot to relax. It's free to access, though you may want to rent a sunbed and umbrella, which

73

typically costs around €10-€15 for the day. There are also small cafes and restaurants nearby where you can grab a bite to eat while enjoying the view.

Another beautiful beach on Paros is Agios Ioannis Beach, located near the village of Marpissa. This beach is more secluded and offers a peaceful atmosphere perfect for swimming, sunbathing, and relaxing in the sun. The clear, calm waters make it an excellent spot for a leisurely swim. The beach is free to access, but there are no facilities, so it's best to bring your own water and snacks. Agios Ioannis is perfect for those looking to escape the crowds and enjoy the island's natural beauty.

Paros also offers great opportunities for outdoor activities, particularly for those who enjoy hiking. The island's diverse landscapes, from the rolling hills to the rugged coastline, offer plenty of trails for hikers of all levels. One popular route is the hike from the village of Lefkes to the village of Prodromos, which takes you through scenic olive groves and traditional villages. The hike is about 6 kilometers long and takes around two hours to complete. It's free to access and offers stunning views of the island and its surroundings.

For a more adventurous experience, consider trying windsurfing or kitesurfing, which are popular activities on

Paros, particularly at Golden Beach. This beach, located on the eastern side of the island, is known for its ideal wind conditions and clear waters, making it one of the top spots in the Cyclades for water sports. There are several companies on the beach that offer lessons and equipment rentals for windsurfing and kitesurfing. Prices typically range from €40 to €70 for a 1-2 hour lesson, depending on the type of activity you choose.

In addition to its beaches and natural beauty, Paros is also home to several important archaeological sites. One of the most significant is the Temple of Apollo, located near the village of Koukounaries. This ancient temple, dating back to the 6th century BCE, was once a major religious center on the island. While the temple is now in ruins, the site offers a fascinating glimpse into Paros' ancient past. The temple is open to visitors year-round and is free to access. The site is quiet and peaceful, making it a great spot for reflection and appreciation of the island's rich history.

Another important archaeological site is the ancient city of Dilion, located on the eastern side of the island. Dilion was an important religious and cultural center in ancient times, and the ruins here include a temple dedicated to the god Apollo. The site is less visited than other archaeological spots on the island, providing a more serene and intimate experience. The site is free to access, and visitors can explore the ruins at their own pace, learning about the island's ancient history.

For those interested in local craftsmanship, Paros is known for its high-quality marble, which has been used for centuries in sculpture and architecture. You can find a number of marble workshops on the island, where artisans create beautiful sculptures, vases, and other decorative pieces. The Parian Marble Workshop in Parikia offers a unique opportunity to see the craftsmanship behind these works and even purchase a piece to take home. Prices for smaller items start around €20, with larger sculptures going for €100 or more.

Milos

Milos, a lesser-known gem in the Cyclades, stands out for its unique landscapes, stunning beaches, and rich history. While it may not have the same level of fame as Mykonos or Santorini, this volcanic island is a true paradise for those looking to explore a more relaxed and unspoiled side of the Aegean. With its strikingly varied geology, crystal-clear waters, and charming villages, Milos offers a captivating mix of natural beauty, history, and culture.

The island's capital, Plaka, is a picturesque town set on a hill, offering stunning panoramic views of the island and the surrounding sea. Plaka is filled with narrow, winding streets that are a joy to wander through, with whitewashed houses, colorful doors, and vibrant bougainvillea. The town is dotted with charming cafes, local shops, and restaurants, where you can sample traditional Greek dishes like moussaka, fresh seafood, and local specialties. One of the main attractions in Plaka is the Venetian Castle, which dates back to the 13th century. The castle is free to visit, and it offers panoramic views of the island, especially at sunset. It's a peaceful spot, perfect for watching the day come to a close while soaking in the island's beauty.

Milos is famous for its beaches, many of which are unlike any others in the Cyclades. Due to its volcanic origin, the island boasts an array of beaches with dramatic landscapes and colorful waters. The most famous of these is Sarakiniko Beach, located on the northern side of the island. With its white, moon-like rock formations and turquoise waters, Sarakiniko has become an iconic spot for photos. The beach is free to access, though it can get crowded during peak season, so it's best to visit early in the morning or later in the evening to avoid the crowds. While Sarakiniko is stunning, it's not ideal for swimming, as the waters are often quite shallow and rocky. However, the area around the beach is perfect for hiking and exploring the unique geological formations.

For those seeking a more relaxed beach experience, head to Firiplaka Beach on the southern coast of Milos. This beach, with its golden sand and crystal-clear waters, offers a peaceful setting for sunbathing and swimming. Firiplaka is well-equipped with sunbeds and umbrellas, which can be rented for around €10-€15 per day. There are also a few small tavernas nearby where you can enjoy a meal with a view of the beach, with prices for a meal typically ranging from €15 to €25 per person. Another beautiful beach worth visiting is Tsigrado Beach, a secluded spot accessible via a steep descent down a rocky path. The effort to reach Tsigrado is well worth it, as the beach is stunning, with clear waters and a peaceful, uncrowded atmosphere. Tsigrado is free to access, but since it's somewhat tricky to get to, it's best to wear sturdy shoes and bring supplies with you.

Milos is also home to some of the most impressive natural landmarks in the Cyclades. The island's volcanic origins have shaped its terrain in fascinating ways, and one of the best ways to explore this is by taking a boat tour around the island. Several companies offer boat trips that take you to hidden coves, caves, and remote beaches, offering a unique perspective on Milos' stunning coastlines. One of the most popular boat trips is the tour to Kleftiko, a sea cave complex with towering rock formations and crystal-clear waters. Kleftiko was once a pirate hideout, and the area is now a protected natural site. Boat tours to Kleftiko typically cost around €40-€60 per person for a half-day trip, with some tours including lunch or snacks. Most boat tours depart from Adamas, the main port of Milos, and are available from April to October.

For a deeper understanding of Milos' history, a visit to the ancient Roman Theater is a must. Located near the village of Tripiti, the theater dates back to the 1st century BCE and could once hold up to 7,000 spectators. The site is free to visit, and it's open daily from 9:00 AM to 7:00 PM. Although much of the theater is in ruins, the surrounding area still offers a fascinating glimpse into the island's past. The nearby Catacombs of Milos, another significant historical site, are considered one of the most important early Christian sites in Greece. The catacombs are located just outside Tripiti and were used as burial sites by early Christians in the 1st-5th centuries CE. Guided tours are available, and entrance fees are typically around €4. The catacombs are open daily from 9:00 AM to 7:00 PM, and a visit offers valuable insight into the island's role in early Christianity.

Another fascinating historical site on Milos is the Archaeological Museum of Milos, located in Plaka. The museum houses a collection of artifacts from the island's ancient past, including pottery, sculptures, and tools from the prehistoric, classical, and Roman periods. The most famous exhibit is the Venus de Milo, a world-renowned statue of Aphrodite that was discovered on the island in 1820 and is now housed in the Louvre Museum in Paris. While the original Venus de Milo is no longer on the island, the museum features replicas and provides a detailed history of the statue's discovery. The museum is open daily from 9:00 AM to 3:00 PM, with an entrance fee of €4. It's a great place to learn about Milos' rich history and the many civilizations that have called the island home.

In addition to its historical and natural attractions, Milos also offers a range of activities for those looking to explore the island's culture and local crafts. The island has a long tradition of pottery-making, and several workshops on the island still produce handmade ceramic pieces using techniques that have been passed down through generations. The Milos Pottery Workshop, located in the village of Plaka, offers visitors the chance to watch artisans at work and purchase unique pottery. Prices for small items like cups or bowls start at around €10-€20, while larger items such as vases or decorative pieces can cost upwards of €50.

Milos is also known for its food, with many restaurants serving delicious Greek dishes made from fresh, local ingredients. A great place to try traditional Greek cuisine is at the taverna "O Hamos," located in the village of Adamas. This family-run restaurant is known for its slow-cooked lamb, moussaka, and fresh seafood, with prices ranging from €15 to €25 per person. Another popular spot in Adamas is "Astakas," which offers seafood dishes like grilled octopus and fried calamari, along with stunning views of the harbor. Prices at Astakas typically range from €20 to €40 per person.

Milos is also an island that thrives on sustainable tourism, with several businesses dedicated to preserving the island's natural beauty and cultural heritage. Visitors are encouraged to respect the local environment by minimizing waste, using eco-friendly products, and supporting local businesses. The island has several small, family-run hotels and guesthouses that focus on providing authentic, sustainable experiences for their guests. Many of these accommodations are located in traditional villages like Plaka or Pollonia, offering a more intimate and eco-conscious alternative to larger resorts.

Ios

Ios, often overshadowed by its more famous neighbors in the Cyclades, is an island that offers the perfect blend of vibrant nightlife, beautiful beaches, and rich history. Whether you're here to soak up the sun, explore ancient ruins, or enjoy the lively atmosphere, Ios has something for everyone.

The main town of Ios, Chora, is a picturesque maze of narrow streets lined with whitewashed houses, vibrant bougainvillea, and small cafes. Chora is the island's heart, offering a lively yet charming atmosphere. It's home to several bars, restaurants, and shops, making it a great place to explore by day and night. The streets are lined with local boutiques where you can pick up handcrafted goods such as leather sandals, jewelry, and pottery. You'll also find quaint cafes offering traditional Greek coffee or refreshing cocktails, perfect for a laid-back afternoon. While Chora's nightlife is a major draw for many, it's also full of peaceful spots for those looking to escape the party scene.

One of the highlights of Chora is the Church of Panagia Gremniotissa, perched at the highest point of the town. The church offers incredible panoramic views of the island, especially at sunset. The hike up to the church is relatively short but steep, and once you reach the top, you'll be rewarded with breathtaking views of the surrounding coastline and the Aegean Sea. The church is open daily, and entry is free. It's a peaceful place to reflect and enjoy the beauty of Ios in a more serene environment.

Just outside Chora, you'll find the Tomb of Homer, which adds an air of mystery to the island's long history. While there is debate over whether Homer, the famed ancient Greek poet, was actually buried on Ios, the site is still of great historical interest. The tomb is thought to be a burial site for an important figure from antiquity and has been a popular spot for visitors for centuries. The site is open daily and free to visit, and it offers a chance to connect with the island's ancient past while surrounded by beautiful views.

Ios is also famous for its stunning beaches, many of which are quieter and less crowded than those on the more tourist-heavy islands. Mylopotas Beach, located just a short walk from

Chora, is one of the most popular and accessible beaches on the island. With its golden sand and clear blue waters, Mylopotas is perfect for swimming and sunbathing. The beach is well-equipped with sunbeds and umbrellas, which can be rented for around €10-€15 for the day. There are also a number of beachfront cafes and tavernas where you can enjoy fresh seafood or a refreshing drink. Prices for a meal typically range from €15 to €30 per person.

For those seeking a more tranquil beach experience, head to Agia Theodoti Beach, located on the island's northern coast. This quieter beach is less developed than Mylopotas, offering a peaceful atmosphere where you can enjoy the sun and sea without the crowds. Agia Theodoti has crystal-clear waters that are perfect for swimming, and the surrounding hills provide a beautiful backdrop. It's free to access, but there are no facilities here, so it's a good idea to bring your own snacks and drinks.

Another beautiful, less-visited beach on Ios is Kolitsani Beach. Situated near Chora, this small, secluded beach offers a peaceful escape, with calm waters ideal for swimming. Kolitsani Beach is free to access and is a great spot to relax if you prefer a quieter atmosphere away from the more popular beaches.

Ios is also known for its impressive hiking trails, which allow you to explore the island's rugged landscape and natural beauty. One of the most popular hikes is the path from Chora to the ancient ruins of Skarkos. This archaeological site features the remains of a prehistoric settlement that dates back to the 3rd millennium BCE. The hike takes about 30 minutes from Chora, and while the ruins themselves are relatively small, the views from the site are spectacular, offering a panoramic view of the island and the surrounding sea. Skarkos is free to visit, and the hike itself is a great way to explore the island's natural beauty. The site is open daily and provides valuable insights into the island's prehistoric past.

For a more extensive hike, consider making your way to the island's highest point, Mount Pyrgos. The hike to the summit takes around 2-3 hours and offers incredible views of Ios and the nearby islands. Along the way, you'll pass through traditional villages, olive groves, and rugged terrain. The hike is free to access, and the panoramic views at the top are well worth the effort.

Ios also offers opportunities for those interested in water activities like windsurfing, kayaking, and snorkeling. Mylopotas Beach is the island's main hub for water sports, with rental shops offering equipment for windsurfing and kayaking. Windsurfing lessons typically start at €40 for a 1-2 hour session, while renting a kayak costs around €10-€20 per hour. The calm, clear waters of Ios make it an ideal destination for these activities, and you'll have the chance to explore the coastline from the sea.

For a deeper dive into Ios' history and culture, the Ios Archaeological Museum in Chora is a great place to learn more about the island's past. The museum features artifacts from the ancient and classical periods, including pottery, sculptures, and tools found on the island and nearby excavations. The museum is open daily from 8:30 AM to 3:00 PM, and the entrance fee is around €2. Visiting the museum provides a great context for understanding the historical sites around the island.

Syros

Syros, the capital of the Cyclades, is an island that offers a perfect blend of historical charm, cultural richness, and vibrant local life. While it may not have the same level of fame as some of the other Greek islands, Syros is a destination that captivates those who visit. Its unique blend of Venetian and neoclassical architecture, combined with the stunning coastal scenery, makes it one of the most beautiful and culturally significant islands in the Cyclades.

The heart of Syros is Ermoupoli, the island's capital and one of the most beautiful towns in Greece. Ermoupoli is a place where history and modern life coexist harmoniously. The town is a masterpiece of neoclassical and Venetian architecture, with grand mansions, ornate churches, and elegant squares. As you wander through the narrow streets, you'll encounter a mix of charming cafes, boutiques, and local shops, offering a taste of the island's vibrant life. The town's atmosphere is relaxed yet lively, making it the perfect place to spend an afternoon exploring.

One of the most striking features of Ermoupoli is its architecture. The town is home to several neoclassical buildings, many of which are located around the central square, Plateia Miaouli. The square is a beautiful example of

Syros' rich cultural heritage, with its grand buildings, including the Town Hall, a neoclassical masterpiece designed by the famous architect Ernst Ziller. The Town Hall, open to visitors during weekdays from 9:00 AM to 3:00 PM, is one of the most impressive buildings in Greece, with its marble façade and intricate details. It's free to visit, and taking a stroll around the square is one of the best ways to admire the town's architecture.

From Plateia Miaouli, head up to the high hill of Ano Syros, the island's medieval district. Here, you'll find a maze of narrow alleys, whitewashed houses, and stunning views over the entire town and the Aegean Sea. Ano Syros is a quiet, traditional area that offers a glimpse into the island's past. At the top of the hill stands the Catholic Cathedral of St. George, which is a must-see. The cathedral, built in the 19th century, is a beautiful example of Catholic architecture and is one of the most important religious sites on the island. The church is open daily, and visitors are welcome to explore the interior, which is adorned with beautiful frescoes and intricate details. There's no entry fee, and it's a peaceful spot to take in the views.

For those interested in the island's rich cultural history, the Archaeological Museum of Syros, located in Ermoupoli, offers an excellent collection of artifacts from the island's ancient past. The museum is housed in a beautiful neoclassical building and features a range of exhibits, from prehistoric pottery to sculptures and tools from the ancient Greek period. The museum is open daily from 9:00 AM to 3:00 PM, and entry costs around €2. It's a great place to get a deeper understanding of the island's history and cultural heritage.

Syros is also known for its festivals, which are a great way to experience the island's lively cultural scene. The most famous of these is the Syros International Film Festival, held every summer. The festival attracts filmmakers and cinephiles from around the world and offers a fantastic selection of films, from indie productions to international cinema. The festival is held in various venues around Ermoupoli, including outdoor cinemas and theaters, and runs for about a week in early September. Tickets typically range from €5 to €10 per screening.

For those who prefer a more relaxed experience, Syros offers a variety of beaches to enjoy. One of the most popular is Galissas Beach, located about 7 kilometers from Ermoupoli. Galissas is a lovely sandy beach with crystal-clear waters, making it perfect for swimming and sunbathing. The beach is lined with cafes, tavernas, and beach bars, where you can enjoy fresh seafood or a cold drink as you watch the waves. Sunbeds and umbrellas can be rented for around €10-€15 per day, and the beach is well-equipped with showers and changing rooms. It's a great spot for families, as the waters are calm and shallow.

Another beautiful beach on Syros is Kini Beach, located on the western side of the island. This beach is known for its tranquil atmosphere and stunning sunsets. Kini has a small fishing village with a few tavernas serving fresh fish, making it a great spot to enjoy a leisurely meal while watching the sunset over the Aegean. The beach is free to access, but sunbeds and umbrellas are available for around €10 per day. Kini is perfect for those looking to relax away from the more crowded beaches.

For those who enjoy hiking, Syros offers several scenic trails that provide stunning views of the island's landscapes and coastline. One of the most popular hikes is the trail from Ermoupoli to the village of Ano Syros, which takes you through traditional neighborhoods and offers panoramic views of the town and surrounding hills. The hike is about 30 minutes and is free to access. Another great trail is the path from the village of Vari to the beach of Megas Gialos. This hike takes you through lush landscapes and offers breathtaking views of the coastline and the Aegean Sea. It's an easy walk, taking about 1.5 hours, and is ideal for those who want to experience Syros' natural beauty on foot.

Syros is also known for its traditional Greek cuisine, and there are many excellent restaurants and tavernas where you can try the island's local dishes. One of the most famous dishes on Syros is "louza," a type of cured pork that is often served with cheese and olives. You can find louza in most local tavernas, and a traditional meal typically costs between €15 and €25 per person. For a truly authentic experience, try "To Tsipouradiko," a small family-run taverna in Ermoupoli known for its fresh seafood and traditional Greek dishes. A meal at To Tsipouradiko will cost around €15-€20 per person, and the friendly atmosphere makes it a great spot to enjoy local food.

For those with a sweet tooth, Syros is famous for its desserts, particularly "syriano," a type of almond-filled pastry that is unique to the island. These sweet treats are often made during special occasions and are a great way to end a meal. The best place to try these local sweets is at "Vrettos," a family-owned patisserie in Ermoupoli that has been serving traditional Syros sweets for generations. Prices for pastries range from €2 to €5, and the shop is open daily from 9:00 AM to 8:00 PM.

Sifnos

Sifnos, a picturesque island in the Cyclades, is an idyllic destination for travelers seeking a blend of traditional Greek charm, stunning landscapes, and rich cultural heritage. While it may not have the same level of fame as Mykonos or Santorini, Sifnos is a hidden gem that has long been a favorite among those who appreciate authentic island life. With its tranquil beaches, charming villages, and excellent cuisine, Sifnos offers a more relaxed, slower-paced experience compared to other islands in the Cyclades.

The island's main town, Apollonia, is a traditional Greek village set in the hills, offering stunning views over the Aegean Sea. Apollonia is the heart of the island, with narrow, winding streets, whitewashed houses, and colorful bougainvillea. As you stroll through the town, you'll encounter charming cafes, local shops, and boutiques selling handmade jewelry, pottery, and textiles. The town is small but lively, and it's the perfect base for exploring the island.

One of the main attractions in Apollonia is the Church of the Seven Martyrs, located on a hill overlooking the town. The church is dedicated to seven Christian martyrs who were executed in the 4th century and is one of the most important religious sites on the island. From here, visitors can enjoy panoramic views of Apollonia, the surrounding hills, and the sea. The church is free to visit, and it's a peaceful spot to reflect and take in the beauty of the island.

Not far from Apollonia is the village of Kastro, an ancient hilltop settlement that is one of the most significant archaeological sites on Sifnos. Kastro was once the island's capital and is home to a number of well-preserved buildings, including old Venetian houses, a medieval castle, and the Church of Panagia, a beautiful whitewashed church that sits at the top of the village. The village offers stunning views over the island and the sea, making it a fantastic spot for photography. Kastro is free to visit, and while it's a relatively quiet spot, it offers a fascinating glimpse into the island's history.

One of the best ways to experience Sifnos' natural beauty is by exploring its hiking trails. The island is known for its well-maintained paths that lead through olive groves, traditional villages, and rugged landscapes. The walk from Apollonia to the village of Artemonas is particularly popular, as it takes you through beautiful countryside and offers incredible views of the island. Artemonas is a charming village known for its well-preserved traditional houses and scenic streets. The village is home to several small cafes and restaurants where you can enjoy local dishes. The hike takes about 30 minutes and is relatively easy, making it suitable for most travelers.

For those who enjoy a more challenging hike, the path to the top of Mount Profitis Ilias is a must-do. At 680 meters, it's the highest point on the island and offers spectacular panoramic views of Sifnos and the surrounding islands. The hike is relatively steep and takes about two hours to reach the summit. Once at the top, you'll be rewarded with breathtaking views of the Aegean Sea, the neighboring islands, and the rugged landscape of Sifnos. The hike is free to access and is an excellent way to experience the island's natural beauty.

Sifnos is also known for its stunning beaches, which offer a mix of relaxed atmospheres and crystal-clear waters. One of the most popular beaches on the island is Vathi Beach, located on the southern coast. Vathi is a sheltered bay with calm, shallow waters, making it ideal for swimming and families with children. The beach is lined with beach bars and tavernas, where you can enjoy a meal or drink while taking in the view. The sunbeds and umbrellas are available for rent at around €10-€15 for the day. Vathi Beach is also a great spot for water sports, such as kayaking and paddleboarding.

Another beautiful beach on Sifnos is Kamares Beach, located near the island's main port. Kamares is a long, sandy beach with crystal-clear waters and a relaxed vibe. It's the perfect place to unwind and enjoy a day at the beach. The beach is free to access, and there are several cafes and tavernas nearby where you can sample fresh seafood and traditional Greek dishes. Kamares Beach is a popular spot for both locals and visitors, but it's never overcrowded, allowing for a more peaceful experience. You can rent sunbeds and umbrellas here for around €10-€15, or simply lay your towel on the sand and enjoy the sun.

For a quieter beach experience, head to Platis Gialos, a small, more secluded beach located on the western side of the island. Platis Gialos is known for its calm waters and relaxed atmosphere, making it an ideal spot for those seeking a more peaceful setting. The beach is surrounded by rocky outcrops, which provide natural shade, and there are a few small tavernas where you can enjoy a meal with a view of the sea. The beach is free to access, and it's a great spot to relax and enjoy the beauty of Sifnos away from the crowds.

Sifnos is also a culinary haven, with a rich tradition of Greek cuisine and local specialties. The island is known for its excellent food, particularly its local dishes made with fresh, locally grown ingredients. One of the island's most famous dishes is "revithada," a slow-cooked chickpea stew that is often served with lamb or pork. The dish is a staple of Sifnos cuisine and is a must-try for anyone visiting the island. Another local specialty is "mousakas," a baked casserole made with layers of eggplant, minced meat, and béchamel sauce. These dishes can be found at many of the island's traditional tavernas and restaurants, where a meal typically costs between €15 and €25 per person.

For a true taste of local Sifnian cuisine, visit the family-run taverna "To Steki," located in the village of Artemonas. This charming taverna is known for its delicious home-cooked meals, including fresh seafood, grilled meats, and traditional Greek appetizers. A meal at To Steki will cost around €20-€30 per person, depending on what you order. Another excellent option in Apollonia is "Kavourmas," a taverna that specializes in local specialties, including revithada and fresh seafood. The atmosphere is relaxed, and the prices are reasonable, with meals typically ranging from €15 to €25.

Sifnos is also famous for its local pottery, which has been made on the island for centuries. The island's pottery workshops offer a chance to see artisans at work, creating beautiful ceramic pieces using traditional techniques. The pottery in Sifnos is known for its simple, elegant designs and is made from local clay that gives the pieces a unique texture. You can purchase pottery at local workshops or shops in Apollonia, where prices for smaller items like cups or bowls start at around €15-€20. Larger pieces, such as vases or decorative bowls, can cost upwards of €50.

For those looking to shop for unique souvenirs, the island also offers a variety of shops selling handmade jewelry, textiles, and other local crafts. One popular shop in Apollonia is "Sifnos Art," which offers a range of locally made jewelry, pottery, and artwork. The shop is open daily and is a great place to find unique gifts to take home.

Amorgos

Amorgos, one of the easternmost islands in the Cyclades, offers an escape from the crowds and a chance to experience a more tranquil, authentic Greek island. Its rugged cliffs, crystal-clear waters, and traditional villages make it an ideal destination for those seeking natural beauty, ancient history, and serene surroundings. Known for its stunning landscapes and well-preserved culture, Amorgos provides a perfect blend of adventure, relaxation, and history.

The island's main town, Hora, is a traditional village that sits perched on a hilltop, offering sweeping views over the Aegean Sea. Hora is the cultural and administrative center of Amorgos, and it's full of charming whitewashed houses, narrow alleyways, and picturesque squares. As you wander through its cobbled streets, you'll encounter local shops, cafes, and restaurants where you can enjoy traditional Greek dishes like moussaka, grilled fish, and local specialties such as Amorgos cheese. The village is relatively quiet, with a relaxed pace of life, and is a great spot to spend an afternoon taking in the peaceful atmosphere.

One of the most iconic sights in Hora is the Monastery of Panagia Hozoviotissa, a must-visit for anyone exploring the island. The monastery, perched on a cliffside 300 meters above the sea, is one of the most important religious sites on the island. Built in the 11th century, it is dedicated to the Virgin Mary and is a striking example of Byzantine architecture. The journey to the monastery involves a steep walk up a series of stairs, but the stunning views of the sea and the surrounding cliffs make it well worth the effort. The monastery is open daily from 8:00 AM to 1:00 PM and 3:00 PM to 7:00 PM, and entry is free, though donations are encouraged. Inside, you'll find a peaceful atmosphere and stunning religious icons that give a glimpse into the spiritual life of the island.

Amorgos is also known for its stunning beaches, which offer a mix of rugged beauty and peaceful surroundings. One of the most popular beaches on the island is Agia Anna Beach, located near the Monastery of Panagia Hozoviotissa. This small, sandy beach is famous for being featured in the 1988 film The Big Blue. The beach is surrounded by steep cliffs, and its crystal-clear waters make it perfect for swimming and snorkeling. It's free to access, and there are a few small cafes nearby where you can enjoy a drink while taking in the view. The beach is relatively quiet, especially in the early morning, making it a great place to relax and unwind.

Another beautiful beach is Mouros Beach, located on the northern side of the island. Mouros is a secluded spot, accessible by a steep path from the village of Aegiali. The beach is small but incredibly beautiful, with calm turquoise waters and dramatic cliffs surrounding it. The area offers an idyllic setting for those looking to escape the crowds and enjoy a peaceful day by the sea. There are no facilities at Mouros Beach, so it's best to bring your own snacks and drinks. The beach is free to access and is perfect for a quiet retreat.

For a more accessible beach, head to Aegiali Beach, located in the village of Aegiali on the island's northern coast. Aegiali is one of Amorgos' largest villages, and its beach is a great place to relax. With its shallow, clear waters, it's ideal for swimming and lounging in the sun. The beach is lined with cafes and restaurants, and sunbeds are available for rent for around €10-€15 per day. Aegiali is a lively village, offering a variety of shops and tavernas where you can sample local dishes. Aegiali Beach is one of the most family-friendly beaches on the island, offering a laid-back atmosphere with plenty of amenities.

For those who enjoy hiking, Amorgos offers some of the most scenic trails in the Cyclades. The island's rugged terrain, dotted with ancient paths and stone walls, makes it a paradise for nature lovers and hikers. One of the most popular hikes is the trail from Hora to the village of Tholaria, which takes you through traditional villages and offers panoramic views of the Aegean Sea. The hike is about 3 kilometers long and takes around an hour, making it suitable for most hikers. The trail is well-marked, and along the way, you'll pass by old stone houses, olive groves, and stunning viewpoints.

Another great hike is the trail to the ancient Minoan site of Minoa, located on a hill overlooking the sea. The hike takes around 30 minutes from the village of Aegiali and offers a chance to explore the ruins of an ancient settlement that dates back to the 3rd millennium BCE. The site is relatively quiet and offers a fascinating glimpse into the island's ancient past. The hike itself is free to access and provides stunning views of the island's coastline.

Amorgos is also home to several interesting archaeological sites, which provide insight into the island's long history. One of the most important sites is the ancient Minoan settlement of Minoa, which was once a thriving town. While much of the site is in ruins, visitors can still see the remains of walls, houses, and a cistern, as well as incredible views over the surrounding area. The site is free to visit and is accessible by hiking trails, making it an excellent way to experience Amorgos' history and natural beauty at the same time.

For a deeper dive into the island's history, visit the Archaeological Museum of Amorgos, located in Hora. The museum is home to a small but significant collection of artifacts, including pottery, sculptures, and inscriptions from the island's ancient and medieval past. The museum is open daily from 9:00 AM to 3:00 PM, and the entrance fee is around €3. It's a great place to learn more about Amorgos' role in ancient Greek civilization and its history over the centuries.

Amorgos is also a fantastic destination for food lovers, with its exceptional local cuisine. The island is known for its fresh seafood, locally grown vegetables, and traditional Greek dishes. One of the most famous dishes on the island is "louza," a cured pork dish that is often served with cheese, olives, and bread. Another local specialty is "rava," a type of sweet semolina cake often served with honey and nuts. You can sample these dishes at one of the island's traditional tavernas, such as "To Steki," located in the village of Aegiali. A meal at To Steki typically costs around €15-€25 per person and offers a fantastic opportunity to try authentic Amorgian cuisine.

For a more upscale dining experience, head to "Katerina's Taverna" in Hora, which is known for its fresh seafood and stunning views over the Aegean Sea. The restaurant serves a range of traditional Greek dishes, including grilled fish, lamb, and moussaka, with prices typically ranging from €20 to €35 per person. The restaurant's terrace offers a wonderful setting for a meal, especially at sunset, when the island is bathed in golden light.

In addition to its excellent food, Amorgos is known for its traditional handicrafts, and you'll find several local shops selling handmade goods such as pottery, jewelry, and textiles. The island is famous for its pottery, which has been made on the island for centuries using traditional techniques. You can visit one of the local pottery workshops, such as "Amorgos Art," located in the village of Tholaria, where artisans create beautiful pottery pieces, including vases, bowls, and plates. Prices for smaller items start at around €15, with larger pieces costing upwards of €50. The workshops offer a chance to see the artisans at work and purchase unique souvenirs to take home.

Tinos

Tinos, one of the lesser-known but profoundly rich islands in the Cyclades, offers an exceptional blend of natural beauty, deep-rooted tradition, and cultural heritage. While it's often overshadowed by its more famous neighbors like Mykonos and Santorini, Tinos is a destination that draws visitors for its unspoiled charm, serene atmosphere, and significant religious importance. The island is perfect for those seeking a blend of history, art, and traditional Greek island life, along with some of the most stunning landscapes in the Aegean.

Tinos is perhaps best known for the Panagia Evangelistria (Church of Our Lady of Tinos), which is one of the most important pilgrimage sites in Greece. Every year, thousands of visitors, particularly Greeks, travel to Tinos to visit the church and pray at the icon of the Virgin Mary, which is believed to have miraculous powers. The church, located in the town of Tinos (the island's main town), is a magnificent example of religious architecture, with its impressive façade, intricate carvings, and grandiose interior. The icon, housed inside the church, is a focal point for pilgrims, who often approach the church on foot, crawling on their knees as an act of devotion.

The church is open daily from 6:00 AM to 9:00 PM, and entry is free. For visitors, it's an awe-inspiring site that embodies the spiritual heart of the island. The surrounding area is also home to the Tinos Archaeological Museum, which displays a collection of artifacts from ancient and Byzantine Tinos, giving insight into the island's rich cultural and religious history. The museum is open from 9:00 AM to 3:00 PM, with an entrance fee of about €3.

Beyond its religious significance, Tinos is also celebrated for its traditional Greek villages, which have maintained their authenticity and charm over the centuries. The island is dotted with quaint villages, many of which are nestled in lush hillsides or perched on rocky outcrops with panoramic views of the sea. One of the most charming villages on Tinos is Pyrgos, located on the western side of the island. Pyrgos is renowned for its marble architecture, as Tinos is famous for its high-quality marble. The village is a center of marble craftsmanship, and many local workshops create intricate marble sculptures, tiles, and even entire buildings. Pyrgos is a picturesque village, with its narrow streets, whitewashed houses, and fountains. It also hosts the Tinos Marble Art Museum, a modern museum dedicated to marble art, displaying works by local and international sculptors. The museum is open from 9:00 AM to 3:00 PM, and the entrance fee is about €4.

Another village worth exploring is Volax, which is unlike any other village on the island due to its unique landscape. Volax is located in the heart of the island, surrounded by giant boulders that create a lunar-like atmosphere. These enormous rocks have made Volax a popular spot for photographers and nature lovers. The village itself is small, but it offers a glimpse into the island's rural life and traditional way of living. The hiking trails around Volax lead to stunning viewpoints and provide a great opportunity to explore the island's diverse flora and fauna. Volax is also known for its basket-making tradition, with several local artisans creating handwoven baskets that make perfect souvenirs.

Tinos is a paradise for hiking enthusiasts, offering a wide range of trails that take you through the island's varied landscapes. The trails pass through traditional villages, ancient ruins, olive groves, and dramatic coastal cliffs, providing a unique way to explore the island. One of the most popular hikes is the trail from Tinos Town to the village of Ktikados, which takes you through beautiful landscapes and offers stunning views of the Aegean Sea. The hike is relatively easy, taking about an hour and a half, and is free to access. Another great trail is the path that leads from the village of Loutra to the isolated beach of Agios Fokas, where you can enjoy a refreshing swim after a rewarding hike. The island is dotted with numerous trails, making it an excellent destination for hiking lovers.

Tinos is also home to some beautiful, more secluded beaches, where you can enjoy a peaceful day by the sea. One of the most popular beaches is Agios Fokas Beach, located just a short distance from Tinos Town. Agios Fokas has clear waters and golden sand, making it a perfect spot for swimming and sunbathing. The beach has sunbeds and umbrellas available for rent at around €10-€15 per day, and there are several beachfront cafes where you can enjoy a meal or a drink with a view of the sea. Another beautiful beach on Tinos is Kolimbithra, located on the northern coast of the island. Kolimbithra is a sandy beach with crystal-clear waters, and it's ideal for swimming and relaxing. The beach is less crowded than Agios Fokas, making it perfect for those who want a quieter beach experience. There are no facilities here, so it's best to bring your own snacks and drinks.

For those looking for a more rugged beach experience, head to Livada Beach, located on the southeastern coast of the island. Livada is a secluded, pebbly beach surrounded by cliffs and rocky formations, offering a peaceful escape from the busier beaches. The beach is free to access, and it's perfect for those looking to enjoy the natural beauty of the island away from the crowds.

When it comes to food, Tinos offers a wealth of delicious local dishes, many of which are made using locally sourced ingredients. One of the island's most famous dishes is louza, a cured pork that is often served with local cheese, olives, and bread. Another popular dish is revithada, a slow-cooked chickpea stew that is a staple of Tinian cuisine. You can find these dishes at many of the island's tavernas and restaurants, with prices ranging from €15 to €25 per person. For a more casual meal, head to one of the local cafes in Tinos Town or Pyrgos, where you can enjoy traditional Greek mezes, such as tzatziki, hummus, and grilled vegetables.

A great spot to try local cuisine is "To Steki," a traditional taverna in the village of Pyrgos. This family-run restaurant is known for its delicious home-cooked meals, including slow-cooked lamb, fresh fish, and vegetarian dishes made with seasonal vegetables. A meal here typically costs around €15-€25 per person, and the atmosphere is welcoming and relaxed. Another excellent option in Tinos Town is "Kavos," a seaside taverna that specializes in fresh seafood and Greek classics. Prices at Kavos usually range from €20 to €30 per person, depending on the dishes you order.

Tinos is also known for its high-quality local products, including olive oil, honey, and traditional sweets. You can visit the local markets or artisan shops to pick up these items as souvenirs. Tinian honey, in particular, is famous for its rich flavor and is often used in local desserts. Many shops in Tinos Town and Pyrgos sell honey, olive oil, and other local products, with prices starting at €5-€10 for small jars.

Serifos

Serifos, a hidden gem in the Cyclades, is a charming and serene island that offers an authentic Greek island experience. While not as well-known as Mykonos or Santorini, Serifos boasts a rugged, untouched beauty with a rich history, picturesque villages, and stunning beaches. Its relaxed pace and stunning landscapes make it a perfect destination for those looking to escape the crowds and immerse themselves in island life.

The island's main town, also called Serifos, is located on a hill overlooking the sea, offering panoramic views of the island's rugged coastline. The town is a maze of narrow streets, whitewashed houses, and vibrant bougainvillea. Serifos Town has a calm and laid-back atmosphere, with local cafes, restaurants, and shops that make for a great place to relax after a day of exploring. As you wander through the cobbled streets, you'll come across traditional tavernas serving fresh seafood, grilled meats, and local specialties. Dining in Serifos is an affordable and authentic experience, with meals typically costing between €15 and €25 per person.

One of the highlights of Serifos Town is the old castle, which sits at the highest point of the town. The castle dates back to the 15th century and offers incredible views of the surrounding island and sea. It's a peaceful spot, with minimal crowds, allowing visitors to take in the panoramic vistas at their own pace. The castle ruins are free to visit, and the walk up to the top is relatively short but steep, making it a great way to stretch your legs and experience some of the island's natural beauty. From the castle, you can see Serifos' beaches, rocky hills, and the Aegean Sea in all directions.

Serifos is also known for its excellent beaches, many of which are still relatively undiscovered by mass tourism. One of the most popular beaches on the island is Livadi Beach, located just a short walk from Serifos Town. Livadi is a beautiful sandy beach with crystal-clear waters, ideal for swimming, sunbathing, and relaxing. The beach is lined with a few cafes and tavernas where you can grab a bite to eat or enjoy a refreshing drink with a view. Sunbeds and umbrellas are available for rent, typically costing around €10-€15 for the day. While Livadi is one of the busier beaches on Serifos, it still maintains a calm and relaxed atmosphere, perfect for those who want to enjoy a peaceful day by the sea.

For a more secluded experience, head to the northern side of the island to the beautiful and remote Psili Ammos Beach. This beach is one of the most stunning on Serifos, with fine golden sand and crystal-clear waters. It's a quiet beach, perfect for those looking to relax and unwind in a peaceful setting. To reach Psili Ammos, you can take a bus or drive, and it's best to arrive early to secure a spot, as the beach is not large and can get crowded during the height of summer. The beach is free to access, but there are no facilities, so make sure to bring your own snacks, drinks, and sun protection.

Another beautiful beach worth visiting is Vagia Beach, located on the eastern coast of the island. Vagia is a small, sheltered beach with soft sand and calm, shallow waters, making it an excellent spot for swimming and families with young children. The beach is free to access and is surrounded by rocky hills that provide a dramatic backdrop. While it's a bit more secluded than Livadi, Vagia still has a laid-back vibe, and there are a few tavernas nearby where you can enjoy a meal with fresh seafood. Sunbeds and umbrellas are available for rent at around €10-€15 per day.

Beyond the beaches, Serifos is a paradise for hikers and nature lovers. The island's rugged terrain is perfect for exploring on foot, with several well-marked hiking trails that take you through rocky hills, traditional villages, and ancient ruins. One of the most popular hikes is the trail from Serifos Town to the village of Koutalas. The hike takes you through olive groves and terraced hillsides, offering stunning views of the island's coastline. The village of Koutalas is a small, peaceful spot where you can stop for a drink or snack before continuing on your hike. The entire hike takes around 1.5 to 2 hours, and the path is well-marked and easy to follow.

Another great hike is the trail that leads to the island's ancient mine ruins. Serifos was once known for its mining activity, and the remains of the old mines can still be explored today. The hike to the mining area takes about 45 minutes and offers a glimpse into the island's industrial past, with impressive views of the coastline and the Aegean Sea. The site is free to visit, and it's an excellent way to combine hiking with a bit of history.

Serifos is also rich in cultural heritage, with several traditional villages that offer a glimpse into the island's history and way of life. The village of Megalo Livadi, located on the southern coast, was once home to a thriving mining community. Today, it's a quiet village with a small harbor and a few cafes where you can enjoy a drink by the sea. The village is home to a small museum that showcases the history of mining on the island, including artifacts and photos from the island's industrial past. The museum is open daily from 9:00 AM to 3:00 PM, and the entrance fee is around €3.

For those interested in the island's religious history, a visit to the Church of Agios Konstantinos in Serifos Town is a must. The church, located on the hill above the town, offers beautiful views of the surrounding area and is a peaceful spot to reflect and enjoy the island's tranquil atmosphere. The church is open daily, and while there is no entrance fee, visitors are encouraged to make a small donation. The church is an excellent example of Serifos' traditional Cycladic architecture and is a reminder of the island's rich religious heritage.

Serifos is also known for its vibrant local food scene, with several tavernas and restaurants serving traditional Greek dishes made with fresh, locally sourced ingredients. The island's cuisine is a mix of Mediterranean flavors, with an emphasis on seafood, fresh vegetables, and locally grown herbs. One of the most popular dishes on Serifos is revithada, a slow-cooked chickpea stew that is a staple of the island's cuisine. Another local specialty is louza, a type of cured pork that is often served with cheese and olives. You can find these dishes at most of the island's tavernas, with prices ranging from €15 to €25 per person for a full meal.

A great place to try local cuisine is "To Steki," a family-run taverna in Serifos Town that serves home-cooked meals made with fresh, local ingredients. The taverna is known for its friendly atmosphere and delicious food, and a meal here typically costs around €15-€25 per person. Another excellent option is "Kavos," a seaside taverna in Livadi Beach, which offers fresh seafood and traditional Greek dishes in a relaxed, beachfront setting. Meals at Kavos usually cost between €20 and €30 per person.

Serifos is also home to several small local shops where you can purchase handmade crafts, such as pottery, jewelry, and textiles. The island is known for its high-quality pottery, and you can visit one of the local workshops to see artisans at work and purchase unique pieces to take home. Prices for smaller items like cups and bowls typically start at around €15, while larger pieces can cost upwards of €50.

Folegandros

Folegandros, one of the more peaceful and undisturbed islands in the Cyclades, provides a genuine and tranquil Greek island experience. Known for its rugged terrain, pristine waters, and untouched charm, Folegandros is a perfect destination for travelers seeking both relaxation and natural beauty. While smaller and less commercialized than its more famous counterparts, Folegandros surprises visitors with its rich history, scenic hikes, and some of the most breathtaking views in the Aegean.

The island's main town, Chora, is a quintessential Cycladic village with narrow streets, whitewashed houses, and vibrant splashes of bougainvillea. Located on a hilltop, Chora offers panoramic vistas of the island and the Aegean Sea. The town exudes a calm and laid-back vibe, making it the ideal place for leisurely exploration. The central square is filled with cozy cafes, traditional tavernas, and small local shops offering everything from handmade jewelry to local delicacies. Dining in Folegandros is a pleasant and relaxed experience, with meals typically ranging from €15 to €25 per person, depending on the dishes.

A must-see in Chora is the Church of Panagia, which stands at the top of the hill above the town. This charming church, dedicated to the Virgin Mary, is one of the island's most significant landmarks. The walk up to the church is a short but scenic journey, with sweeping views of the town below and the surrounding hills. The church itself is simple yet striking, with a peaceful ambiance perfect for quiet contemplation. Open daily and free to visit, the church offers a serene break from the hustle and bustle of daily life.

Folegandros is renowned for its natural landscapes, and hiking is one of the best ways to appreciate the island's beauty. There are several well-marked trails that lead through olive groves, traditional villages, and rugged cliffs, offering stunning views of the coastline and the Aegean Sea. One of the most popular hikes is the trail from Chora to the impressive Church of the Seven Martyrs, perched on a cliff overlooking the sea. The walk takes about 30 minutes and rewards hikers with incredible panoramic views. The church itself is small but historic, making it a perfect spot for reflection and photos.

The island also offers some of the best beaches in the Cyclades, each with its own unique charm. One of the most popular beaches is Agali Beach, located just a short distance from Chora. This sandy beach is sheltered by cliffs and has calm, clear waters, making it perfect for swimming and sunbathing. Agali is also home to a few beachfront tavernas where you can enjoy local seafood or a cold drink while relaxing by the sea. Sunbeds and umbrellas are available for rent for around €10-€15 per day. Agali Beach is a great choice for families, as the waters are shallow and safe for children.

For a more secluded beach experience, head to the small but stunning Katergo Beach, accessible only by boat or a steep hiking path. The beach is known for its crystal-clear waters and tranquil atmosphere. It's an ideal spot for those looking to escape the crowds and enjoy a peaceful day by the sea. The beach is free to access, but there are no facilities, so it's best to bring your own snacks and water. The hike to Katergo Beach is a bit challenging, but the reward is worth it — the beach offers a perfect setting for a quiet retreat, surrounded by dramatic cliffs and crystal-clear waters.

Another quiet beach on the island is Livadi Beach, which is also near Chora. Livadi is a small sandy beach with calm, shallow waters and a relaxed atmosphere. It's ideal for swimming or simply lounging by the water. The beach is less crowded than Agali or Katergo, offering a more peaceful experience. There are a few small cafes nearby, and sunbeds and umbrellas can be rented for around €10-€15 per day. Livadi Beach is the perfect spot for those seeking a more tranquil setting, away from the busier beaches.

The island's rugged landscape and serene beaches make it an excellent place for outdoor activities beyond hiking and swimming. Folegandros is an ideal destination for those who enjoy exploring nature at their own pace. If you're interested in exploring more remote areas of the island, consider renting a scooter or ATV to access some of the more secluded spots. Many of the island's beautiful beaches, such as Katergo, are only accessible by boat or hiking, and having the flexibility to explore at your own pace enhances the experience.

Folegandros also has a fascinating history and culture, which visitors can learn more about by exploring its museums and archaeological sites. The Folegandros Folklore Museum, located in Chora, offers a glimpse into the island's past, with exhibits showcasing traditional artifacts, tools, and household items from past centuries. The museum is open daily from 9:00 AM to 2:00 PM, with an entrance fee of around €2. For those interested in ancient history, the island's ancient ruins at the site of Kastro are a must-see. These remnants of a medieval settlement are perched on a hill overlooking the sea, providing both historical insight and breathtaking views.

One of the island's unique cultural aspects is its connection to local artisans and traditional crafts. Folegandros is known for its pottery, weaving, and embroidery. Visitors can find many small shops around Chora and the villages, offering handmade ceramics and textiles. These items make excellent souvenirs, and purchasing them directly from local artisans ensures that you're supporting the island's traditional craftsmanship. Prices for smaller pottery items typically start at €15, while larger, more intricate pieces can range from €40 to €100.

For food lovers, Folegandros offers a variety of delicious local dishes, with fresh seafood and local ingredients taking center stage. One of the island's specialties is matsata, a traditional pasta dish served with a rich meat or seafood sauce. You can also try revithada, a hearty chickpea stew that's a staple of the island's cuisine. Folegandros' cuisine reflects the simple, rustic charm of the island, with an emphasis on fresh, local produce. A great place to enjoy these dishes is "To Steki," a small family-run taverna in Chora that offers delicious home-cooked meals. Meals here typically range from €15 to €25 per person. For a more upscale experience, visit "Katergo," a seaside restaurant located near the beach, where you can enjoy fresh fish and Mediterranean dishes with a view of the sea. Prices at Katergo usually range from €25 to €40 per person.

In addition to its wonderful cuisine, Folegandros is also known for its wines, produced on the island from local grape varieties. The island's vineyards are small but produce high-quality wines, and many tavernas and restaurants offer local wines by the glass or bottle. One of the best places to sample local wines is at the "Folegandros Winery," which offers wine tastings and tours of its vineyards. The winery is open from 10:00 AM to 6:00 PM, and tastings typically cost around €10-€15 per person.

Koufonisia

Koufonisia, a pair of small islands nestled in the Cyclades, provides a rare escape from the bustle of the more famous Greek destinations. The islands—Koufonisi and Kato Koufonisi—are known for their idyllic beaches, crystal-clear waters, and quiet charm. They offer a genuine Greek island experience where the pace of life slows down, making it an ideal destination for those seeking relaxation, natural beauty, and a more authentic slice of island life.

Koufonisi's main village, also called Koufonisi, is a small and picturesque settlement located right on the water's edge. The village has a laid-back atmosphere, with whitewashed houses adorned with colorful shutters and blooming bougainvillea. As you walk along the narrow streets, you'll come across several cafes and tavernas offering local dishes made with fresh, seasonal ingredients. Koufonisi is small enough that you can walk from one end of the village to the other in less than 10 minutes, but its peaceful charm and welcoming locals make it a perfect spot to spend a few days.

One of the first places you'll likely notice when you arrive on the island is the harbor, where small fishing boats and water taxis dock. From here, you can take a boat trip to the nearby beaches, as well as to the neighboring island of Kato Koufonisi, which remains largely uninhabited and is known for its tranquil beauty. The boats are available throughout the day, and prices typically range from €10-€15 for a round-trip fare. The trips are short and provide a fantastic opportunity to experience the crystal-clear waters and rugged beauty of the island from the sea.

The main attraction of Koufonisia, however, lies in its beaches. The island is home to some of the most stunning, untouched beaches in the Aegean. Pori Beach, located on the southern coast, is perhaps the most famous. With its powdery white sand and turquoise waters, Pori is often described as one of the best beaches in Greece. The beach is perfect for sunbathing and swimming, and the waters are calm and shallow, making it ideal for families and those seeking a relaxing day by the sea. There are no beach bars or sunbeds here, giving Pori a more natural and unspoiled feel. The beach is free to access, though there are no facilities, so it's recommended to bring water, snacks, and any necessities you might need for the day.

Another stunning beach on Koufonisi is Finikas Beach, located on the opposite side of the island from Pori. Finikas is a quieter, more secluded beach with soft sand and shallow waters perfect for swimming. Unlike Pori, Finikas is lined with a few tavernas where you can enjoy fresh seafood or a cold drink while taking in the views. Sunbeds and umbrellas are available to rent for around €10-€15 per day. The peaceful atmosphere of Finikas Beach makes it a favorite for those looking for a quieter place to relax.

For a more isolated experience, head to Italida Beach, a small cove accessible by a short hike or boat ride. Italida is one of the more remote beaches on the island, and it offers a more intimate beach experience. The waters here are calm, and the beach is surrounded by rocks and cliffs that provide natural shade. Like many of the other beaches on Koufonisi, Italida remains relatively undeveloped, and it's the perfect spot for those looking to escape the crowds and enjoy some solitude.

Beyond the beaches, Koufonisia offers plenty of opportunities to explore its natural beauty. Hiking is a great way to take in the island's stunning landscapes, and several trails lead through rocky terrain, olive groves, and hills dotted with traditional windmills. One of the most popular hikes is the trail from the village to the island's highest point, where you'll be rewarded with panoramic views of the Aegean Sea and the surrounding islands. The hike is free to access and offers a great way to experience the island's natural beauty up close.

Andros

Andros, one of the northernmost islands in the Cyclades, offers visitors a more serene and authentic Greek island experience, far from the heavy tourist crowds of its more famous counterparts. The island, with its lush landscapes, traditional villages, and historical landmarks, is perfect for those seeking a blend of natural beauty, culture, and adventure.

The island's main town, also called Andros, is a picturesque blend of Venetian and neoclassical architecture, with narrow streets, marble-paved squares, and charming old houses. Andros Town, often referred to as Chora, is the island's bustling center, offering visitors a range of activities and attractions. The town's central square, Plateia Mita, is surrounded by cafes, restaurants, and shops where you can enjoy a leisurely meal or shop for local products. The vibrant atmosphere is perfect for those who want to soak in the island's charm while tasting traditional Greek dishes or enjoying a cool drink in one of the many outdoor cafés.

One of the most prominent attractions in Chora is the Archaeological Museum of Andros, located near the town center. This museum houses a significant collection of artifacts from the ancient and medieval periods of the island, including pottery, sculptures, and tools from the island's long history. The museum's most famous exhibit is the 2,500-year-old statue of the "Goddess of Andros," which was discovered on the island and provides valuable insight into its ancient past. The museum is open daily from 9:00 AM to 3:00 PM, and admission is around €3. It's an excellent stop for anyone interested in exploring the island's rich cultural heritage.

For another taste of Andros' history, a visit to the Andros Museum of Modern Art is a must. Located just a short walk from the main square, the museum houses a unique collection of Greek modern art, with works by some of the country's most celebrated artists. The museum is open daily from 10:00 AM to 2:00 PM and from 5:00 PM to 9:00 PM, with an entrance fee of €5. Its picturesque location, surrounded by olive trees, adds to the charm of the experience, offering both art lovers and casual visitors an opportunity to discover contemporary Greek creativity.

Another fascinating historical site on the island is the Monastery of Panagia Tourliani, located just outside of Chora in the village of Messaria. The monastery, dating back to the 16th century, is dedicated to the Virgin Mary and is one of Andros' most important religious sites. The beautiful whitewashed church and its impressive marble iconostasis make it a lovely place to visit for those interested in history or architecture. The monastery is open daily from 8:00 AM to 1:00 PM and from 4:00 PM to 7:00 PM, and entry is free. The monastery is surrounded by lush gardens, offering visitors a peaceful and serene atmosphere.

Andros is known for its diverse landscapes, from green hills and valleys to rugged coastal cliffs, making it a perfect destination for hikers. The island is crisscrossed with well-marked trails that take you through picturesque villages, olive groves, and scenic viewpoints. One of the best hikes on the island is the route from Chora to the village of Stenies. The trail takes you through a stunning natural landscape, offering breathtaking views of the sea, the surrounding islands, and the mainland. The village of Stenies is known for its traditional stone houses and charming atmosphere, making it an excellent spot to take a break and enjoy a meal at one of the local tavernas. The hike typically takes around an hour and a half and is relatively easy, making it accessible for most hikers.

For more adventurous trekkers, the trail that leads to the island's highest peak, Mount Petalo, is a must-do. The hike to the summit takes around 3-4 hours, but the panoramic views of the island, the surrounding sea, and the nearby islands are well worth the effort. The mountain is dotted with wildflowers and offers a stunning display of Andros' natural beauty. The path is steep in places, so it's best to bring sturdy footwear and plenty of water. The hike is free to access and provides a true sense of adventure and connection with the island's rugged landscape.

Andros is also famous for its beautiful beaches, many of which are quieter and more peaceful than the more tourist-heavy spots in the Cyclades. One of the most popular beaches on the island is Agios Petros, located on the island's southern coast. Agios Petros is a long, sandy beach with clear waters, ideal for swimming and sunbathing. The beach is well-equipped with sunbeds and umbrellas for rent, typically costing €10-€15 per day. The beach is also lined with tavernas and beach bars, where you can enjoy fresh seafood and Greek dishes while taking in the view. Agios Petros is a great spot for families or anyone looking for a beach with easy access to amenities.

For a more secluded beach experience, head to the northern part of the island to the quiet and pristine beach of Gialia. Gialia is less developed than Agios Petros, offering visitors a peaceful and relaxing environment. The beach is free to access, and while there are no facilities, its crystal-clear waters and scenic surroundings make it a perfect spot to unwind. The beach is ideal for swimming and picnicking, especially if you're looking to escape the crowds. The serene atmosphere of Gialia makes it one of the most tranquil beaches on Andros.

Another beautiful beach worth visiting is Batsi Beach, located in the village of Batsi on the western side of the island. Batsi is a charming seaside village with a lovely beach that offers both shallow and clear waters. It's the most popular beach on Andros, but it's still quiet compared to those on more tourist-heavy islands. The beach is lined with cafes and tavernas serving traditional Greek dishes, and you can rent sunbeds and umbrellas for around €10-€15. The village of Batsi is also a great spot to enjoy a stroll along the harbor, which is dotted with colorful fishing boats.

Andros is also home to a thriving culinary scene, with a variety of traditional tavernas serving local specialties. One of the island's most famous dishes is revithada, a chickpea stew that is slow-cooked to perfection. You can find revithada at most local tavernas, often served with a side of fresh bread and olive oil. Another local specialty is louza, a cured pork that is typically served with olives and cheese as a meze. You'll find these dishes and more at local favorites like To Steki in Chora, where a meal typically costs around €15-€25 per person.

For those interested in exploring the island's local products, the small village of Korthi offers an excellent spot to shop for handmade goods. Local artisans in Korthi create beautiful pottery, textiles, and jewelry that make for unique souvenirs. You'll find a number of small shops selling these handmade items, as well as locally produced honey, olive oil, and herbs.

The island is also home to several cultural festivals, which provide a deeper insight into the island's traditions and way of life. One of the most popular events is the Andros International Festival, which takes place every summer and includes a variety of cultural performances, from traditional music and dance to theatrical productions and art exhibitions. The festival is a wonderful way to experience the local culture and meet the island's friendly residents.

Antiparos

Antiparos, a small island in the Cyclades, is known for its peaceful atmosphere, crystal-clear waters, and traditional Greek charm. Despite its proximity to Paros, it remains relatively undiscovered by mass tourism, offering a serene retreat for those looking to enjoy the unspoiled beauty of the Aegean. The island combines natural beauty with a laid-back village atmosphere, making it an ideal destination for a relaxing escape.

The main village, Antiparos Town, is a charming labyrinth of narrow streets, whitewashed houses, and vibrant flowers. It's the island's heart, where most of its shops, restaurants, and cafes can be found. As you wander through the village, you'll notice the gentle pace of life. People chat casually in the cafes, and the scent of fresh bread from the bakeries fills the air. While there are no grand attractions in the town, its quiet charm and simple beauty are its biggest draw. Stopping by a café in the central square for a coffee or Greek pastry is the perfect way to soak up the atmosphere. A typical meal in Antiparos Town costs around €15-€25 per person, depending on where you dine.

One of the main draws of the island is its beaches. Antiparos is home to some of the most beautiful, uncrowded beaches in the Cyclades, with fine sand and clear, turquoise waters. Psaraliki Beach, one of the most popular on the island, is located just a short walk from Antiparos Town. This beach has calm waters, perfect for swimming and snorkeling. There are also a few beach bars where you can rent sunbeds and umbrellas for around €10-€15 for the day. Psaraliki is a favorite spot for families, offering a relaxed atmosphere, and while it gets busier during the peak summer months, it's still far less crowded than the beaches on other nearby islands.

For those seeking a more secluded beach, Agios Georgios Beach on the southern tip of the island is a great option. This beach offers a peaceful setting, with minimal development. It's the perfect place to unwind and enjoy the natural beauty of Antiparos. The beach is free to access, and while there are no amenities here, its calm waters and quiet atmosphere make it a great spot to escape the crowds. The drive to Agios Georgios Beach takes around 15 minutes from the main village, but the journey is well worth it for the serene setting.

Another beautiful, lesser-known beach is Livadia, located to the west of the island. This small, sandy beach is surrounded by steep cliffs and is relatively untouched by tourism. While there are no sunbeds or umbrellas for rent, the beach is perfect for those looking for some solitude by the sea. You can access Livadia Beach by foot or a short drive from the town, and once you arrive, you can spend your time swimming, lounging, or simply enjoying the natural surroundings.

Beyond its beaches, Antiparos offers a wealth of outdoor activities for those keen to explore the island's diverse landscapes. The island is small and relatively flat, making it ideal for cycling. Renting a bike for the day usually costs around €10-€15, and the bike-friendly roads allow visitors to easily explore the island at their own pace. You can cycle from Antiparos Town to the villages of Agios Georgios or even to the nearby caves.

The Cave of Antiparos, located just outside the main village, is one of the island's most fascinating natural attractions. The cave, discovered in the early 19th century, is known for its stunning stalactites and stalagmites. The cave stretches deep into the hillside, and a guided tour will take you through its striking chambers. The tour lasts about 45 minutes, and the cave's entrance fee is €5. The cool interior offers a refreshing break from the island's heat, and the formations inside are truly impressive. The cave is open daily from 9:00 AM to 6:00 PM, making it a great stop on a day of exploring.

Antiparos is also home to several ancient ruins that offer a glimpse into the island's long history. One of the most significant historical sites is the Temple of Apollo, located near the cave. This ancient temple dates back to the 6th century BCE and was dedicated to Apollo, the Greek god of music and prophecy. While only the foundations and some columns remain, the site offers an interesting peek into Antiparos' religious and cultural history. The Temple of Apollo is free to visit and is open throughout the year, making it a great spot for history enthusiasts or anyone interested in the island's ancient past.

If you enjoy hiking, the island offers a number of scenic trails that take you through its rolling hills, olive groves, and rocky outcrops. One of the best hikes is the trail that leads from Antiparos Town to the old Venetian castle ruins, which date back to the 15th century. The castle is perched on a hill and offers panoramic views of the surrounding islands. The hike takes about an hour and is moderate in difficulty, making it accessible to most visitors. The ruins are free to explore and are a peaceful spot to take in the surrounding landscape. Along the way, you'll pass by traditional houses and small chapels, adding to the charm of the hike.

For those seeking more water-based activities, Antiparos offers excellent opportunities for kayaking, paddleboarding, and snorkeling. The island's calm, clear waters are perfect for exploring, and you can rent equipment from one of the local shops or beach bars. Kayaking or paddleboarding around the coastline allows you to access hidden beaches and coves that can't be reached by land. Rental prices for a kayak or paddleboard are usually around €15-€25 per hour, depending on the location.

When it comes to dining, Antiparos offers an excellent selection of tavernas, many of which specialize in fresh seafood. One of the most popular spots is To Souvlaki, a casual taverna near the harbor. Here, you can enjoy a variety of grilled meats, seafood, and traditional Greek dishes. Meals at To Souvlaki typically cost between €15 and €25 per person. For a more refined experience, head to Barbouni, a seaside restaurant offering fresh fish and Mediterranean specialties. Located near Psaraliki Beach, Barbouni provides a picturesque setting with prices typically ranging from €25 to €40 per person.

If you're interested in trying something local, make sure to sample amygdalota, an almond-based sweet that is a traditional Antiparos treat. Many of the local bakeries sell these delicate, sugary bites, which are perfect for enjoying with a cup of coffee or taking home as a souvenir. A box of amygdalota usually costs around €8-€12.

For those who enjoy shopping, Antiparos offers a variety of small boutiques and artisan shops selling handmade jewelry, pottery, and textiles. The island's shops offer a great selection of locally crafted goods, including beautiful ceramic items, handwoven fabrics, and intricately designed jewelry. Prices vary, with smaller items like rings and necklaces starting at around €15, while larger pottery pieces can range from €30 to €60. These unique, handcrafted pieces make for the perfect souvenir to remember your time on the island.

Antiparos is also home to several festivals and cultural events throughout the year. One of the most popular is the Antiparos Festival, held in the summer. The festival features local music, traditional dances, and theater performances, offering a wonderful opportunity to experience the island's rich cultural heritage. The festival typically takes place in late July or early August, and the events are free to attend. It's an excellent way to immerse yourself in the local culture and meet the friendly islanders.

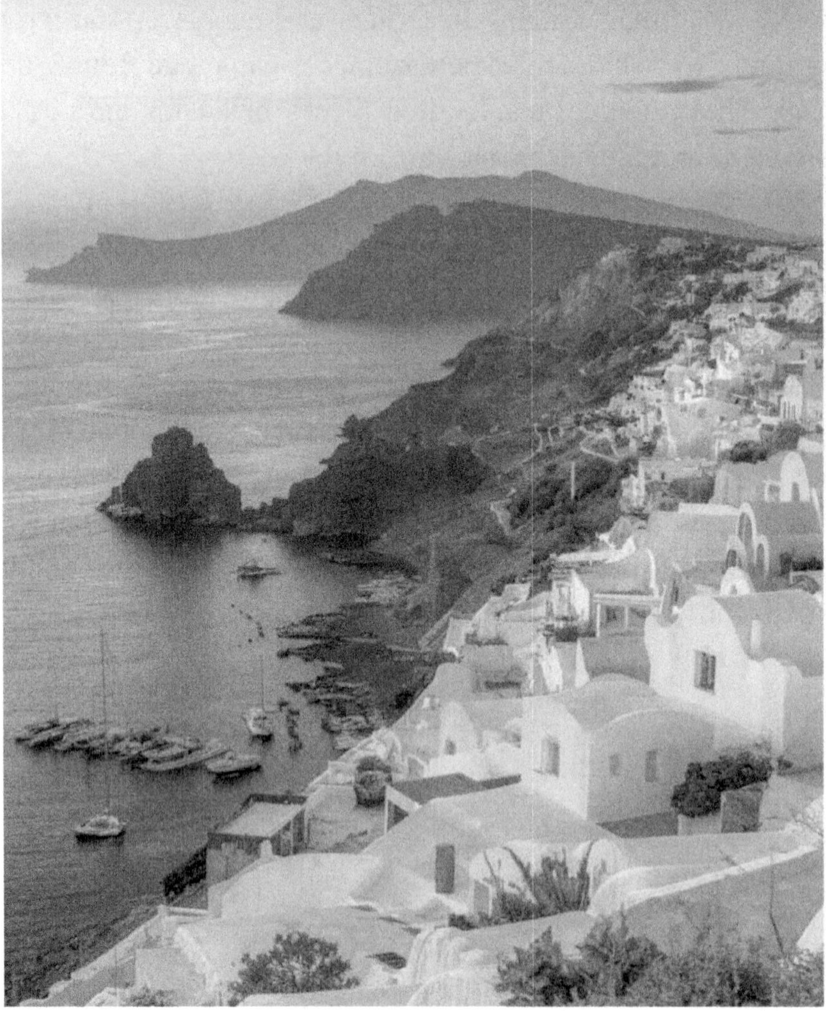

Culture & Traditions

Historic Sites & Museums

The Cyclades are renowned for their captivating beauty, but beyond their beaches and vibrant villages lies a rich history waiting to be explored. The islands boast a wealth of historical sites and museums that offer a glimpse into their fascinating past, from ancient ruins to Byzantine monuments, reflecting the diverse cultures that have shaped the region over the centuries.

On the island of Delos, one of the most important archaeological sites in Greece, history is alive in its vast ruins. Delos was once a thriving religious center, dedicated to Apollo, and served as a bustling port city before its decline in the 3rd century BCE. Today, the island is an archaeological park, where visitors can wander through the remains of temples, houses, and public spaces. Among the most significant sites is the Temple of Apollo, which was once the heart of the island's worship, along with the Sacred Way, leading up to the temple, lined with statues of lions, some of which have been restored. The archaeological site is open daily from 8:00 AM to 3:00 PM, with an entrance fee of €12. A boat trip from Mykonos to Delos typically costs around

€20-€30, and it's highly recommended to spend at least three hours exploring this UNESCO World Heritage site. It's a journey back in time, as the sprawling ruins offer a glimpse of ancient Greek religion, art, and daily life.

Mykonos, known for its beaches and nightlife, also offers historical attractions for those willing to dive into its past. The Archaeological Museum of Mykonos, located in the heart of Mykonos Town, houses a collection of artifacts from the island's ancient history, including pottery, sculptures, and tools found on nearby islands and in the surrounding waters. Highlights include the famous "Mykonos Vase," depicting scenes from Greek mythology. The museum is open every day from 9:00 AM to 3:00 PM, with an entrance fee of €6. Not far from the museum, the Folklore Museum offers insight into the island's more recent history, showcasing traditional Mykonian life with exhibits of local textiles, household items, and tools. It's open from 10:00 AM to 2:00 PM, and entry costs around €3.

On Paros, history is woven into the island's everyday fabric. The Archaeological Museum of Paros in Parikia houses a remarkable collection of ancient artifacts, with highlights including the Parian Marble, which dates back to the 3rd century BCE and was used for some of the island's most significant statues. The museum's exhibits focus on the island's ancient past, including pottery, sculptures, and artifacts from the early Christian and Byzantine periods. The museum is open daily from 8:30 AM to 3:00 PM, with a modest entrance fee of €4. Another must-see site on Paros is the Church of Panagia Ekatontapiliani, also known as the Church of the Hundred Doors. This Byzantine church, dating back to the 4th century, is one of the best-preserved early Christian churches in Greece. The church is free to visit, and while the interior is simple, the history of its construction and the role it played in the Christianization of the island is fascinating.

Naxos, the largest island in the Cyclades, is rich in archaeological sites. The most famous landmark is the Portara, the massive marble doorway that once led to the Temple of Apollo, built in the 6th century BCE. The entrance, which remains a striking symbol of Naxos' ancient history, overlooks the harbor and is especially dramatic at sunset. Visitors can reach the Portara by walking from Naxos Town, and there is no fee to visit. Naxos also offers the Archaeological Museum of Naxos, which holds a collection of artifacts from the island's ancient past, including statues, pottery, and inscriptions from the Classical and Hellenistic periods. The museum is open every day from 9:00 AM to 3:00 PM, with an entrance fee of €3.

For those interested in the more recent history of the Cyclades, the Museum of the Cycladic Art in Athens offers an incredible collection of art and artifacts from the early Cycladic period. Though not located in the islands themselves, this museum is essential for understanding the rich prehistory of the Cyclades. The collection includes famous marble figurines from the 3rd millennium BCE, including the iconic Cycladic figurines that are known worldwide. The museum is open daily from 10:00 AM to 5:00 PM, with an entrance fee of €10.

On Tinos, the Museum of Marble Crafts showcases the island's long history of marble carving. Tinos is renowned for its marble, which has been used for centuries in sculpture and architecture. The museum highlights the importance of marble craftsmanship and offers a unique insight into the skills of local artisans. The museum is located in the village of Pyrgos, open every day from 9:00 AM to 3:00 PM, and the entrance fee is €4. Pyrgos itself is a charming village filled with marble houses and sculptures, making it a great place to wander and take in the island's artistic heritage.

In Folegandros, the small Folklore Museum is worth a visit for those interested in the island's more recent history. The museum showcases traditional island life, from agricultural tools to clothing and household items, reflecting the simpler ways of life that once dominated the island. Folegandros also has a small but fascinating Castle, located in the town of Chora. Built in the 12th century to defend the island from pirate raids, the castle ruins offer beautiful views of the island's rugged landscape. The castle is free to visit and is a peaceful spot for visitors to enjoy the island's charm.

In Sifnos, the Archaeological Museum of Sifnos is located in the main town, Apollonia, and contains a variety of finds from the island's long history, including ancient pottery, sculptures, and jewelry. One of the highlights is a collection of pottery from the early Cycladic period, reflecting the island's importance as a center for pottery production. The museum is open daily from 9:00 AM to 3:00 PM, with a small entrance fee of €2.

One of the most impressive museums in the Cyclades is located on Kea. The Archaeological Museum of Kea is home to several important finds, including sculptures from the ancient city of Ioulis. The museum focuses on Kea's role in ancient Greece, showcasing items that span from the prehistoric to the classical period. The museum is open daily from 9:00 AM to 3:00 PM, and the entrance fee is typically around €3. Kea's ancient ruins, including the Temple of Athena, are worth exploring, and the island's peaceful atmosphere makes it a perfect destination for history enthusiasts.

In Syros, the Museum of Industrial History offers insight into the island's past as a major industrial center. The museum, housed in a former soap factory, traces the island's industrial heritage, including shipbuilding, soap making, and textile production, which were vital to Syros during the 19th and 20th centuries. The museum is located in Ermoupolis, the island's capital, and is open Monday to Saturday from 10:00 AM to 4:00 PM, with an entrance fee of €5.

Local Festivals

The Cyclades are home to a rich tapestry of local festivals that celebrate everything from religious traditions to ancient rituals and modern arts. These festivals offer a unique opportunity to immerse yourself in the island culture, providing visitors with the chance to experience the islands in their most vibrant, festive forms. Whether you're witnessing a religious procession in Tinos, enjoying local music on Naxos, or attending a culinary festival in Paros, the festivals of the Cyclades create an atmosphere of togetherness, tradition, and joy.

One of the most famous festivals in the Cyclades is the Panagia Evangelistria Festival in Tinos, which takes place annually on August 15. This religious festival honors the Virgin Mary and is one of the most important celebrations in Greece. Pilgrims from all over Greece come to Tinos to pay homage to the Virgin Mary, believed to possess miraculous powers. The celebration begins with a procession from the port to the Panagia Evangelistria Church, where the faithful walk barefoot, some crawling, as an act of devotion. The church, with its grand façade and majestic interior, becomes a place of worship and reflection for thousands. The festival is a mix of solemn religious rituals and lively celebrations, including music, dancing, and traditional food. Many tavernas around the island serve special dishes during this period, with the prices of meals typically ranging from €20 to €30 per person. The church is open daily, but during the festival, the atmosphere becomes incredibly charged with spiritual energy. This event provides a deeply moving experience that connects you with the heart of the island's religious traditions.

In Mykonos, a more cosmopolitan flair is added to the local festival calendar with the Mykonos Biennale, held every two years. The event spans several weeks and brings together artists from around the world to showcase modern art in various forms, from visual arts to performances and installations. The festival takes place in various venues across

Mykonos, including galleries, open-air spaces, and even on the beaches. It's an artistic celebration that allows visitors to engage with cutting-edge creativity, often in unexpected locations. The festival is a fantastic way to experience the island's blend of tradition and contemporary culture. It typically takes place in September and is free to access for many of the public exhibitions. For performances and special events, tickets can range from €10 to €25. The biennale brings a fresh, vibrant atmosphere to the island, making it a great time to visit if you appreciate art and culture.

On Naxos, the Festival of Naxos held in July is a highlight of the island's cultural calendar. This festival celebrates the island's deep musical and cultural heritage, featuring performances of local music, dance, and theater. One of the standout features is the Naxos Classical Music Festival, which brings classical musicians to the island to perform in the grand Basilica of Agios Nikolaos and other historical venues around the island. The combination of classical music set against the backdrop of Naxos' ancient ruins and natural beauty creates a captivating experience. Many of the performances are free to attend, though more formal events can require tickets ranging from €15 to €30. The festival is a great opportunity to experience the island's artistic side while enjoying its historical charm.

In Paros, the Paros International Documentary Festival stands out as a major cultural event. Held annually in July, the festival screens a wide variety of international documentaries in both indoor and open-air venues. Paros' intimate setting makes it an excellent location for a festival that emphasizes thought-provoking narratives and storytelling. The festival is free to access for many public screenings, though special film premieres or workshops may require tickets ranging from €5 to €15. During the event, Paros becomes a hotspot for cinephiles and creative minds, and you can also enjoy discussions with filmmakers, panels, and special events.

Another festival on Paros that draws visitors is the Feast of the Assumption of the Virgin Mary, held on August 15, celebrated in the village of Marpissa. This religious festival involves processions, music, dancing, and feasts. The highlight is the evening celebration in the village square, where the community gathers to share traditional food and enjoy folk music. Expect to pay between €15 and €25 for a meal during the festival, where local specialties like souvlaki, moussaka, and revithada (chickpea stew) are served in abundance. The energy of this celebration provides an immersive experience of Paros' vibrant local culture, with music echoing through the night and the festive atmosphere lingering long into the evening.

On Ios, the Ios Festival held each August is a lively celebration of the island's youth culture and rich musical history. The festival features live performances, including rock and electronic music, and often attracts young crowds looking to enjoy the island's more laid-back yet vibrant vibe. Ios is known for its nightlife, and this festival combines the island's party atmosphere with its deep cultural traditions. The festival also includes art exhibitions, local crafts, and food stalls. It's a great festival for those who want to experience the island's lively social scene, with tickets for most events ranging from €10 to €20. Ios' stunning beaches and sunset views also provide the perfect backdrop to this youthful, energetic celebration.

In Sifnos, one of the quieter islands in the Cyclades, the Festival of Sifnos held in August offers a mix of traditional music, folk dances, and theater performances. The highlight of the festival is the Sifnos Folklore Dance Night, where locals and visitors alike come together to dance to traditional Greek tunes. The event is a great way to experience the island's slower, more intimate rhythms, with festivities centered around the village squares. A meal during the festival costs between €15 and €30, and you'll likely find a menu filled with traditional Sifnian dishes like mastelo, a slow-cooked lamb dish that is a local specialty. The festival is free to attend, but tickets for specific performances or activities may vary.

On Folegandros, the Feast of the Assumption of the Virgin Mary on August 15 is another religious festival that combines devotion with celebration. Folegandros' festival is particularly special because it takes place in the village of Chora, and it's a much more local and intimate experience compared to larger islands. The festival includes a religious procession to the church, followed by traditional music, folk dancing, and plenty of food. The celebration is marked by a communal spirit, and meals served at the local tavernas typically cost between €15 and €25. The lively yet traditional atmosphere is a great way to experience the island's deep-rooted customs.

On Tinos, which is known for its religious significance, the Tinos Pilgrimage (held annually on August 15) is the island's most significant festival. The event honors the Virgin Mary and is one of Greece's most important religious celebrations. Pilgrims from all over the country visit Tinos to venerate the icon of the Virgin Mary, believed to have miraculous powers. The pilgrimage is both a spiritual journey and a cultural event, as locals and visitors gather to participate in church services, processions, and folk music performances. Many tavernas in Tinos offer special meals during the festival, with prices typically ranging from €20 to €30 per person for a traditional Greek feast.

In Kea, the Kea Cultural Festival held each summer showcases the island's local traditions through music, theater, and art performances. The festival brings together both local talent and international artists to perform at various venues around the island, including the open-air theater in Korissia. It's an excellent way to experience the cultural richness of Kea, and many of the events are free to attend, though some performances or exhibitions may require a small fee. The festival's relaxed nature and blend of arts make it a must-see for those who want to experience the quieter side of the Cyclades, away from the more tourist-heavy islands.

Village Life

In the Cyclades, village life presents a beautiful, authentic experience that showcases the simplicity and charm of traditional Greek living. Unlike the bustling tourist hubs, these villages offer a slower pace, where time seems to stand still, and the rhythm of daily life is dictated by the natural surroundings and centuries-old traditions.

On the island of Paros, the village of Naoussa is a fantastic example of how village life blends the old with the new. Naoussa, once a sleepy fishing village, has blossomed into a charming town that still retains its traditional character. The harbor is lined with quaint whitewashed houses and fishing boats bobbing in the water. Here, fishermen still bring in their daily catch, and the smell of freshly prepared seafood wafts from the local tavernas, many of which have been passed down through generations. While there are a few upscale restaurants along the waterfront, the heart of Naoussa remains deeply rooted in the island's traditions, and meals in the tavernas typically range from €15 to €25 per person. For a true taste of local life, stop by one of the local markets selling fresh produce, cheeses, and handmade goods. The market operates daily from early morning until 1:00 PM, and it's an excellent opportunity to interact with locals and pick up some souvenirs.

Moving to Tinos, the village of Pyrgos is one of the best places to experience authentic island life in the Cyclades. Known for its marble craftsmanship, Pyrgos has retained its traditional character with stone-paved streets, narrow alleys, and beautiful marble houses. The village is also home to the Museum of Marble Crafts, where visitors can learn about the history of marble carving on the island. The museum is open daily from 9:00 AM to 3:00 PM, with an entrance fee of €4. As you wander through Pyrgos, you'll encounter artisans working in their studios, creating intricate marble sculptures and pieces of art that have made Tinos famous. The village is quiet, offering a perfect escape to witness everyday life. The smell of freshly baked bread and local pastries fills the air from the small bakeries, and the community's sense of pride in its heritage is palpable.

In Mykonos, a place renowned for its nightlife and beaches, Ano Mera offers a refreshing glimpse into traditional village life. Located in the center of the island, Ano Mera is a stark contrast to the bustling streets of Mykonos Town. The village square is peaceful, with a few cafes and tavernas where you can enjoy a leisurely meal and chat with the locals. At the heart of Ano Mera is the Monastery of Panagia Tourliani, a 16th-century monastery that adds a spiritual and historical dimension to the village. The monastery is open daily from

8:00 AM to 1:00 PM and 4:00 PM to 8:00 PM, with free admission. It's a calm, reflective spot where you can witness the peaceful rhythm of daily life in the village, away from the island's tourist crowds.

On Naxos, the village of Apeiranthos is a standout destination for those wanting to experience a more remote, authentic side of island life. Nestled high in the mountains, Apeiranthos is known for its stone-paved streets, traditional whitewashed houses, and welcoming locals. The village is rich in history, and its isolated location has helped preserve its unique culture. The village is famous for its marble streets, and the houses are built with local stone, giving it an earthy, rustic feel. Apeiranthos is home to a number of small museums, such as the Archaeological Museum of Apeiranthos, which showcases the island's long history, with exhibits ranging from prehistoric artifacts to Byzantine relics. The museum is open daily from 9:00 AM to 2:00 PM and charges a small fee of €2 for entry. The village's tranquility and its agricultural surroundings, including olive groves and vineyards, provide visitors with a genuine insight into rural life in the Cyclades. For a taste of local food, try the village's signature dish, "kavourmas," a type of pork preserve, which you can find in the local tavernas.

Folegandros offers another exceptional example of traditional village life. The island is small, but its charm lies in the simplicity of its villages. Chora, the island's capital, has a slow-paced rhythm, with its narrow, winding streets leading to whitewashed houses and cozy tavernas. The village square is often filled with locals chatting over coffee, and the sound of clinking glasses and the smell of grilling meats fills the air as night falls. Folegandros' sense of community is strong, and the people here take pride in their island's traditions. The tavernas serve simple, fresh food, such as grilled meats, seafood, and "fava," a type of split pea puree that's a staple on the island. Dining in Folegandros usually costs around €20-€25 per person. The island's pace is set by the sun and the sea, with few distractions, making it a perfect place to experience life as it was before the influence of mass tourism.

On Kea, the village of Ioulis offers visitors a wonderful opportunity to experience traditional island life. The village, perched on a hill, has been wonderfully preserved, with its stone-built houses and charming narrow lanes. Ioulis is the ancient capital of the island, and much of the village's appeal lies in its historical context. The village is car-free, which only adds to its charm, as pedestrians stroll through the quiet streets. A visit to the Archaeological Museum of Kea will give you a glimpse into the island's past, with exhibits that focus on Kea's ancient role in Greek history. The museum is open daily from 9:00 AM to 3:00 PM, with an entrance fee of €3. In Ioulis, you'll find small local shops selling handmade goods, including pottery and textiles, perfect for taking home a piece of the island's culture.

Antiparos, though small, also provides an authentic view of island life. The village of Antiparos Town is compact but lively, with its whitewashed houses and narrow streets leading to the island's vibrant port. The pace of life here is leisurely, and much of the island's economy is based on fishing and agriculture. The harbor is a great place to watch local fishermen bringing in their daily catch, which is then sold in the town's markets and used in the local tavernas. Dining in Antiparos is typically relaxed, with many of the tavernas offering simple, delicious meals. You can expect to pay around €15-€20 for a meal of freshly caught fish and locally produced vegetables. The quiet nature of Antiparos makes it a great place to enjoy slow walks around the village, taking in the natural beauty and the authentic Greek village atmosphere.

On Sifnos, Artemonas offers a picturesque glimpse into traditional island life. The village is known for its cobbled streets, vibrant bougainvillea, and well-preserved neoclassical houses. It's a peaceful, residential village with a strong community spirit. The local bakeries serve fresh bread and pastries, while small shops sell handcrafted pottery and textiles. Dining here is centered around traditional Greek food, with many local tavernas offering specialties like mastelo (lamb cooked in wine). A typical meal in Artemonas will cost between €15 and €25 per person, and the village is known for its exceptional local cuisine.

Syros, the administrative capital of the Cyclades, is home to Ano Syros, a medieval hilltop village that provides a fascinating window into island life through the ages. This village, steeped in history, is characterized by its narrow, labyrinthine streets and Venetian architecture. Ano Syros offers a slower pace, where locals still carry out daily activities much as they have for centuries. The Catholic Church of St. George, perched atop the hill, is one of the highlights of the village and offers stunning views over the island. It's free to visit, though donations are appreciated. While in Ano Syros, make sure to stop by the local cafes and bakeries, which serve traditional Greek sweets and coffee, offering an authentic taste of local life.

Artisan Workshops

The Cyclades are not just known for their stunning landscapes and beaches but also for their rich tradition of craftsmanship. Across the islands, artisan workshops offer visitors the opportunity to witness firsthand the skills and techniques that have been passed down through generations. From pottery and textiles to marble carving and jewelry-making, these workshops provide a window into the soul of island life, where art is not just something you admire but something that is intricately woven into the fabric of daily existence.

On Tinos, artisan workshops are particularly famous for marble carving. Tinos has long been a center for marble craftsmanship, and many workshops on the island continue to produce stunning marble sculptures, both traditional and modern. The village of Pyrgos is at the heart of this craft, home to numerous marble studios and galleries. As you wander through Pyrgos, you'll encounter workshops where skilled artisans create everything from delicate figurines to large-scale statues, using marble sourced directly from the island. The Museum of Marble Crafts in Pyrgos (open daily from 9:00 AM to 3:00 PM, entrance fee €4) provides an excellent introduction to the island's marble-working history and its role in shaping the Cycladic identity. If you're interested, some workshops offer demonstrations where you can watch the craftsmen at work, or even try your hand at carving a small piece. These workshops often sell pieces ranging from €10 for small decorative items to several hundred euros for larger sculptures.

Paros is another island where artisan craftsmanship thrives, particularly in pottery. The Paros Pottery Workshops in Margarita and Naoussa give visitors the chance to experience the island's ancient pottery tradition. Pottery in Paros dates back thousands of years, and these workshops continue to produce traditional designs alongside more modern pieces. The workshops are a great place to learn about the methods of handcrafting clay, from shaping the pots on the wheel to glazing and firing them in traditional kilns. You can buy beautifully crafted pottery items, ranging from €10 for small decorative items to €50 and up for larger, intricately designed pieces. Some workshops also offer pottery classes, where you can get hands-on experience with the craft. The workshops typically operate daily from 10:00 AM to 6:00 PM, and prices for a class range from €30 to €50 per session, depending on the complexity of the lesson.

On Naxos, the island's marble tradition is also significant, with workshops that focus on creating marble art and functional objects. Naxos marble is renowned for its fine quality, and local artisans use it to craft everything from sculptures to functional items such as tables and sinks. Filoti, a traditional village on the island, is home to several workshops where visitors can see marble being carved into beautiful shapes. Many workshops in Naxos also offer lessons in marble carving and sculpture, allowing you to learn from experienced artisans. The prices for a marble sculpture can range from €50 for small pieces to €500 or more for large sculptures. Visiting these workshops gives you a sense of the labor and skill that goes into producing these timeless works of art.

Mykonos may be known for its nightlife, but the island also has a growing arts and crafts scene. In Ano Mera, you can find artisan workshops focusing on leather goods, particularly handmade sandals. Mykonos is famous for its leather sandal-making tradition, and several workshops on the island produce high-quality, custom-made sandals that are perfect for the hot summer months. You can visit these workshops and watch as the artisans craft sandals from scratch, often with a choice of designs and colors. These leather sandals, starting at around €30, are both stylish and comfortable and make for an excellent souvenir from your trip. Many of these workshops offer the chance to design your own pair, with prices varying based on customization.

On Syros, the Syros Leather Workshop offers a fascinating experience for anyone interested in the island's craftsmanship. Located in Hermoupolis, Syros' capital, this workshop specializes in handcrafted leather bags, belts, and shoes. The leather goods here are made using traditional techniques passed down through generations, and the finished products are known for their quality and durability. You can find anything from wallets and purses to larger items like handbags and belts. Prices for leather goods typically range from €30 for small items like wallets to €100 for larger, more intricate pieces. The workshop is open daily, from 10:00 AM to 5:00 PM, and visitors are often welcome to watch the artisans at work or even participate in short leather-working classes for a small fee.

Sifnos is a quieter island that boasts a long tradition of food and textile craftsmanship. Local Sifnian ceramics are highly regarded for their delicate, hand-painted designs, and the island's workshops allow you to observe the whole process of creating these beautiful pieces. Kamares, the main port, is home to several pottery workshops where you can see artisans shaping clay into vases, bowls, and decorative items, often inspired by the island's natural landscape. A ceramic vase from Sifnos typically costs between €15 and €40, depending on the size and intricacy of the design. Visitors can also take pottery classes in some workshops, with prices typically ranging from €25 to €40 per session. These workshops are open daily, and many of them sell pottery directly from the studio, allowing you to take home a handmade souvenir that reflects the island's artistic heritage.

Folegandros, with its stunning natural beauty, is also home to a number of artisan workshops focused on textiles. The island has a history of weaving, and many workshops continue to produce beautiful, handwoven items like scarves, tablecloths, and blankets using traditional techniques. The weaving process is labor-intensive and requires skill and patience, making the finished pieces not only beautiful but also a testament to the island's craft traditions. Prices for handwoven textiles typically range from €20 to €50, depending on the complexity of the design. These workshops offer a chance to see the artisans at work and to purchase high-quality, locally made textiles.

In Antiparos, artisan workshops are often small family-run businesses where visitors can watch craftsmen working with wood, creating everything from furniture to decorative items. The workshops focus on sustainable practices, using locally sourced wood and traditional methods to create functional yet beautiful pieces. Prices for wooden objects like chairs or tables can range from €50 for smaller items to several hundred euros for larger, custom-made pieces. These workshops often offer visitors the chance to see how the pieces are made and learn about the island's woodworking tradition.

Hidden Treasures

The Cyclades are renowned for their stunning landscapes and rich history, but beyond the well-known attractions, the islands hold hidden treasures waiting to be discovered by those willing to venture off the beaten path. From remote beaches to secluded villages, these hidden gems offer a more intimate and authentic glimpse of the islands, away from the bustling crowds and tourist hotspots. Exploring these lesser-known treasures provides an opportunity to connect with the Cyclades' true essence, experiencing a slower pace of life and a sense of serenity that is often missed in the more popular areas.

On Tinos, one of the islands most celebrated for its religious significance, there are hidden corners that many visitors overlook. The village of Kardiani, located in the island's mountainous interior, offers a peaceful retreat surrounded by lush greenery. This village, built into the slopes of Mount Tsiknias, is characterized by its traditional stone houses, narrow streets, and stunning views over the Aegean. Walking through Kardiani feels like stepping back in time, with little to disturb the village's peaceful rhythm. Here, you can wander through the alleys, enjoy a drink at a local café, and admire the beautiful views without the throngs of tourists. The village is also known for its authentic tavernas, where you can enjoy traditional Tinian dishes such as louza (cured pork) and kavourmas (spiced pork preserve), typically costing €15-€20 per person.

Another hidden gem on Tinos is the Monastery of Kechrovouni, perched high in the hills above the village of Volax. This serene, ancient monastery is often missed by tourists but offers a quiet place for reflection and stunning panoramic views of the island and the surrounding sea. The monastery is free to visit, though donations are encouraged. It's a peaceful spot to witness the spiritual side of Tinos and enjoy the quiet, isolated atmosphere that contrasts with the hustle and bustle of the island's main town.

On Paros, the village of Marpissa is one of the most charming and least visited by tourists. Nestled in the island's southern hills, Marpissa is a picturesque village full of narrow cobblestone streets, whitewashed houses, and blooming bougainvillea. The village feels like a step back in time, and its tranquility is a welcome respite from the more popular spots on Paros. Marpissa is also home to the Church of Agios Ioannis and several small Byzantine-era chapels, offering a glimpse into the island's rich religious history. A visit to the village can be combined with a hike to the nearby Mount Prophet Elias, which offers stunning views of the island's southern coastline. In the evening, the village square comes alive with locals gathering for coffee or dinner at the small tavernas, where meals typically cost between €15 and €25 per person.

Naxos, the largest island in the Cyclades, is home to the village of Apiranthos, a true hidden treasure that often flies under the radar. This mountain village, built of marble, is a labyrinth of narrow streets, stone houses, and charming corners. Apiranthos is known for its rich history, including its connection to the ancient island of Naxos and its tradition of marble carving. Visitors can explore the village's small museums, such as the Archaeological Museum of Apiranthos, which displays artifacts from the ancient city of Naxos. One of the best ways to experience Apiranthos is by simply wandering through the village, taking in its beautiful architecture, and chatting with the locals. You can also stop for a meal at one of the tavernas, which offer hearty local fare like revithada (chickpea stew) and kakavia (fish soup), for around €15-€20.

In Mykonos, a destination famous for its cosmopolitan vibe, there are still hidden treasures to discover. One such place is the quiet village of Ano Mera, located in the island's interior.

While Mykonos Town is known for its nightlife and beaches, Ano Mera offers a stark contrast with its peaceful atmosphere, traditional Cycladic architecture, and slower pace of life. The village is home to the Monastery of Panagia Tourliani, a 16th-century monastery that offers a serene environment for reflection. The monastery is open daily from 8:00 AM to 1:00 PM and 4:00 PM to 8:00 PM, and it's free to visit. The surrounding area is ideal for hiking, with paths leading to secluded beaches like Fokos Beach, which remains relatively untouched by the crowds. Fokos is a pristine beach with soft sand, clear water, and no facilities, making it a great spot for those looking to escape the crowds. It's accessible by a short drive from Ano Mera, with parking available.

On Sifnos, one of the quieter and less touristy islands in the Cyclades, the village of Kamares is a tranquil treasure waiting to be explored. The village is known for its picturesque setting along a bay, with its whitewashed houses and blue-domed churches. Kamares is also home to several artisan workshops, where visitors can watch local craftspeople at work, creating pottery, textiles, and other traditional products. A short hike from Kamares will lead you to the Kamares Beach, a peaceful spot with soft sand and clear water, ideal for swimming or simply relaxing. For a more remote experience, take a hike to Chrysopigi Monastery, which offers breathtaking views of the sea and surrounding landscape. The monastery is free to visit, and the hike takes about 45 minutes.

In Folegandros, the village of Chora is a hidden gem with its narrow, winding streets, whitewashed houses, and dramatic clifftop views. The village feels more like a retreat than a tourist destination, with a relaxed atmosphere and a strong sense of community. Folegandros is also known for its charming local shops and artisan studios, where you can buy handmade jewelry, pottery, and other crafts. The island is home to Panagia Church, a beautiful church perched on a cliff that offers panoramic views of the island. The church is free to visit and provides a peaceful spot to reflect while taking in the surrounding beauty. From Chora, you can also hike to the Katergo Beach, one of the island's most secluded beaches, where the journey itself is part of the adventure. The hike takes about 30 minutes, and the beach is a pristine, tranquil spot perfect for those seeking solitude.

On Antiparos, the island's peaceful atmosphere and quiet village life make it a hidden treasure in itself. Antiparos Town is a small, quaint village with narrow streets and whitewashed buildings, offering a perfect escape from the more tourist-heavy islands. The village is home to several artisan workshops, where you can watch locals create pottery, jewelry, and other handcrafted goods. The Cave of Antiparos is another must-see, a natural wonder with impressive stalactites and stalagmites that have been forming for centuries. The cave is open daily from 9:00 AM to 6:00 PM, and the entrance fee is €5. Visitors can take a guided tour through the cave, which lasts about 45 minutes, offering a glimpse into the island's geological history. Antiparos also boasts several beautiful, secluded beaches, including Agios Georgios Beach, a serene spot with crystal-clear waters and no facilities, providing the perfect opportunity for relaxation.

Outdoor Adventures

The Cyclades offer an abundance of outdoor adventures, with each island showcasing its unique natural beauty. Whether you're looking to explore rugged coastlines, hike through ancient landscapes, or take in the serenity of secluded beaches, these islands provide the perfect playground for outdoor enthusiasts. The diversity of terrain, from steep cliffs and rolling hills to tranquil waters, ensures that there's something for everyone seeking adventure and nature.

On Naxos, the largest island in the Cyclades, hiking is a popular way to explore its varied landscapes. One of the most rewarding hikes is the trail that leads from Chora, the main town, to the Temple of Demeter, which dates back to the 6th century BC. The 45-minute walk through ancient olive groves and rocky paths offers stunning views of the island's fertile valleys and mountains. The ruins of the temple, surrounded by wildflowers and ancient stone walls, provide a glimpse into Naxos' past. The hike is free to enjoy, and the temple itself is open to visitors year-round. For more serious hikers, Naxos offers trails that take you up to Mount Zas, the highest peak in the Cyclades. The trek to the top can take around three hours, but the panoramic views of the Aegean Sea and surrounding islands are worth the effort. The path can be rocky and challenging, so it's recommended to wear sturdy footwear and bring water. The best time to hike is early in the morning or late afternoon to avoid the midday heat.

Paros offers a different kind of outdoor adventure, particularly for those who love exploring by bike. The island's relatively flat terrain makes it perfect for cycling, and several cycling routes weave through picturesque villages, vineyards, and sandy beaches. One of the most popular cycling routes takes you from Parikia, the island's capital, to Naoussa, a charming village on the northern coast. Along the way, you can stop at Kolymbithres Beach, famous for its smooth granite rocks and crystal-clear waters, perfect for a refreshing swim after your ride. Bike rentals are widely available in Paros, with prices typically ranging from €15 to €25 per day, and many rental shops offer guided tours of the island. The route from Lefkes, an inland village known for its traditional architecture, to the coast also provides a unique opportunity to see the island's interior, dotted with ancient olive trees and traditional stone houses.

On Mykonos, beyond its vibrant nightlife and famous beaches, there are opportunities for outdoor adventures as well. The island's rugged landscape and steep hills make it a great place for hiking, with several well-marked trails offering spectacular views. One of the most popular hiking routes is the path that leads from Ano Mera to the Monastery of Panagia Tourliani, a peaceful 16th-century monastery. The walk takes about an hour and offers scenic views of the surrounding countryside. After visiting the monastery, hikers can continue toward the remote Fokos Beach, a quiet, unspoiled spot with crystal-clear waters, perfect for a swim. The hike to Fokos is moderate, taking around two hours, and is a great way to enjoy Mykonos' natural beauty away from the crowds. Many of the trails on Mykonos are free to access, and a simple map can guide you to some of the best spots.

For those seeking a more coastal adventure, Ios offers plenty of opportunities for kayaking and stand-up paddleboarding. Manganari Beach, located on the island's southern coast, is one of the best spots for water sports. The beach is known for its calm, shallow waters and is perfect for kayaking, especially for beginners. Rental shops on the beach offer equipment for as low as €15 per hour. Paddling along the coastline provides a unique perspective of Ios' dramatic cliffs and hidden coves. If you prefer something more challenging, several tour operators offer guided sea kayaking trips to explore the island's secluded beaches and caves. These tours typically cost between €30 and €50 per person, depending on the length of the trip.

On Tinos, the landscape invites exploration by foot, and there's no better way to experience the island's rural beauty than by hiking its many trails. One of the best-known routes is the trail from Tinos Town to the village of Kardiani. This path takes you through olive groves, dry-stone walls, and lush vegetation, with views of the Aegean and the nearby islands. The village of Kardiani, nestled into the hills, offers a quiet escape, and its traditional stone houses and narrow lanes add to its charm. The hike takes about an hour, and the trail is free to walk. For a longer trek, the route to the Monastery of Kechrovouni, perched high on a mountain, is a rewarding challenge. The monastery is a peaceful place to rest and take in the sweeping views of the island below. The hike to Kechrovouni takes around two to three hours, and the monastery is open to visitors daily from 8:00 AM to 1:00 PM and 4:00 PM to 7:00 PM.

For water sports enthusiasts, Antiparos offers fantastic opportunities for diving and snorkeling. The island is surrounded by crystal-clear waters teeming with marine life, making it a perfect place to explore the underwater world. The Cave of Antiparos, with its crystal-clear waters and dramatic formations, is a popular diving site. Many local dive shops offer guided tours to the cave, with prices ranging from €40 to €60 for a 45-minute dive. Snorkeling is also a popular activity, especially around the small islets near the island, where you can swim with schools of fish and explore underwater caves. The beaches around Antiparos are quieter than those on nearby Paros, giving you the chance to enjoy the natural beauty of the island in peace.

Kea, also known as Tzia, is another island with fantastic hiking opportunities. Kea's lush landscape, dotted with wildflowers, ancient ruins, and tranquil beaches, makes it an ideal destination for hikers. One of the most scenic hikes on the island is the trail to the Kea Lighthouse, located on the northern tip of the island. The lighthouse offers stunning views of the surrounding sea and nearby islands. The hike is moderate and takes about an hour, with a mix of coastal paths and rocky terrain. The island also offers several other hiking trails, many of which lead to remote beaches or ancient ruins. Hiking in Kea is free to enjoy, and there are plenty of paths that are easily accessible without a guide.

On Folegandros, hiking is one of the best ways to discover the island's raw beauty. The Chora to Katergo Beach hike is particularly popular, taking you from the village of Chora down to one of the island's most secluded beaches. The path is relatively easy but offers breathtaking views of the rugged coastline and deep blue sea. The hike takes about 30 minutes, and the beach is a peaceful spot to relax and swim. For a more challenging adventure, consider hiking up to the Panagia Church, located at the top of a cliff. The panoramic views from the church, especially at sunset, are unforgettable. The hike takes about an hour, and the church is open daily for visitors.

Family Activities

In the Cyclades, families will find an abundance of activities that perfectly blend relaxation, adventure, and cultural exploration. The islands offer something for everyone, from relaxing on family-friendly beaches to visiting ancient sites and experiencing local traditions. Whether you're looking to enjoy nature, indulge in outdoor activities, or discover the history and culture of the islands, the Cyclades provide an ideal setting for family vacations.

On Naxos, the largest island in the Cyclades, families can explore the Portara, the massive marble doorway that is one of the island's most famous landmarks. The short walk to the site is ideal for families with young children, offering stunning views of the sea and surrounding countryside. The Portara is located just outside Naxos Town, and there is no entry fee, making it an easy and accessible attraction for all. After visiting the Portara, families can head to the Agios Georgios Beach, located nearby, for a day of sandcastle-building and swimming. The beach is shallow, making it safe for children to play, and there are plenty of cafes and beach bars where you can relax while keeping an eye on the little ones. Sunbeds and umbrellas are available for rent, typically costing €10-€15 per day.

If your family enjoys hiking, the Temple of Demeter is another family-friendly attraction on Naxos. Located in the village of Sangri, this 6th-century temple is an easy hike from the nearby village. The trail winds through olive groves and ancient fields, offering a fun and educational walk for children. The temple is free to visit, and the surrounding area is perfect for a picnic. The path is well-marked and relatively flat, making it accessible for families with children of all ages.

Paros also has several family-friendly activities, particularly on its quieter beaches. Kolymbithres Beach, located in the northwest of the island, is famous for its unique granite rock formations that create natural swimming pools. The shallow waters here are perfect for younger children, and the smooth rocks offer a safe environment for them to explore. The beach has basic facilities, including sunbeds and umbrellas, and there are a few cafes nearby serving snacks and refreshments. Rental prices for sunbeds and umbrellas are around €10-€15 for the day.

Another excellent family destination on Paros is Paros Park, a protected natural area on the island's northern coast. The park is home to a number of easy hiking trails that are perfect for families, offering stunning views of the sea and surrounding countryside. There's also a small amphitheater in the park where local performances, including children's theater, are occasionally held during the summer months. Entry to the park is free, and it's a great spot for families to enjoy a day outdoors with a picnic or a swim in the crystal-clear waters of Lageri Beach, located nearby.

On Mykonos, families can spend a day at the Mykonos Folklore Museum to experience the island's traditional life. The museum, located in Mykonos Town, has exhibits on everything from the island's history to its folk arts and crafts. The museum is small and easy to explore with children, offering a fun and educational experience. The museum is open daily from 10:00 AM to 2:00 PM, and the entrance fee is typically €3. The museum is a great way to introduce younger visitors to the rich history of Mykonos.

For a day out in nature, Ano Mera is a family-friendly village that offers a quiet escape from the bustle of Mykonos Town. The village is home to the Monastery of Panagia Tourliani, which dates back to the 16th century. The monastery is an excellent spot for a leisurely walk and offers beautiful views of the island's countryside. The monastery is open daily from 8:00 AM to 1:00 PM and from 4:00 PM to 8:00 PM, and it's free to visit. After exploring the monastery, families can stop for a meal at one of the local tavernas, many of which offer traditional Greek food that kids will love.

On Tinos, the island's beautiful beaches offer plenty of opportunities for family fun. Agios Fokas Beach is one of the most popular spots for families, with calm waters perfect for swimming and shallow areas where younger children can play. The beach is located about 2 km from Tinos Town and is well-equipped with sunbeds and umbrellas, available for around €10-€15 per day. After spending time at the beach, families can explore the village of Kardiani, one of the island's most picturesque villages, known for its traditional architecture and narrow streets. It's a great spot for a peaceful walk, and there are local shops and cafes where you can enjoy refreshments.

For a more educational experience, the Tinos Archaeological Museum provides insight into the island's ancient history. Located in Tinos Town, the museum displays artifacts from the island's ancient past, including sculptures, pottery, and inscriptions. The museum is open daily from 10:00 AM to 2:00 PM and has an entrance fee of about €4. The museum is a wonderful way to introduce children to the ancient world while enjoying a cool, quiet space.

In Ios, families will find a relaxed environment perfect for enjoying the outdoors. Manganari Beach, located on the island's southern coast, is a beautiful, quiet beach with shallow waters, ideal for young children. The beach is accessible by car or bus, and it's less crowded than the more popular beaches on the island, providing a peaceful atmosphere for families. The beach has no facilities, so it's best to bring your own food and drinks for a family picnic. For a more exciting day, families can take a boat tour around the island, with various operators offering half-day excursions that cost between €25 and €50 per person. These tours typically stop at secluded beaches and offer opportunities for swimming and snorkeling.

Kea offers a more rural and tranquil experience for families, with plenty of opportunities to explore nature. The island's numerous hiking trails are perfect for families who want to spend a day outdoors. The trail to the Kea Lighthouse provides beautiful views of the island's coastline and is an excellent option for families with older children. The hike takes about an hour and is moderate in difficulty, but the stunning views of the Aegean Sea make it worth the effort. Kea also has many hidden beaches, like Koundouros Beach, which is quieter and less developed than some of the other beaches in the Cyclades, making it a peaceful spot for families to relax.

On Sifnos, the village of Kamares offers a relaxed atmosphere and a family-friendly beach. Kamares Beach is one of the most accessible beaches on the island, with shallow waters perfect for young swimmers. The beach has a few cafes and restaurants where families can enjoy a meal, and sunbeds and umbrellas are available for rent at around €10-€15 for the day. After a day on the beach, families can visit the Archaeological Museum of Sifnos, which is located in the village of Apollonia. The museum offers exhibits on the island's ancient history and is a great way for children to learn about the island's past. The museum is open daily from 9:00 AM to 3:00 PM, with an entrance fee of about €2.

In Folegandros, families can enjoy a quiet, scenic day in Chora, the island's main town. The town is known for its cobbled streets, whitewashed houses, and stunning views of the sea. Chora is car-free, making it a peaceful place to wander with children. The town square is the perfect spot to relax and enjoy a coffee or snack while watching local life unfold. From Chora, families can take a short hike to Katergo Beach, a secluded cove with soft sand and crystal-clear waters. The hike takes about 30 minutes, and the beach offers a serene escape from the crowds.

Nightlife & Entertainment

The Cyclades, known for their idyllic beaches and charming villages, also boast a vibrant nightlife scene that caters to every taste, whether you're looking for lively bars, intimate tavernas, or energetic beach clubs. Each island offers its own unique blend of entertainment, from traditional Greek music to modern beats, ensuring there's something for everyone after the sun sets.

On Mykonos, the nightlife is legendary, attracting visitors from around the world for its high-energy clubs and glamorous beach parties. The heart of Mykonos' nightlife is Mykonos Town, with its narrow streets lined with bars, restaurants, and nightclubs. Here, the party doesn't stop until dawn, and you'll find a variety of venues to suit your mood. For those looking for a chic night out, Cavo Paradiso is a must-visit. Perched on a cliff overlooking the sea, this world-famous club plays host to some of the world's top DJs and offers unforgettable sunset views. The entrance fee typically ranges from €30 to €50, depending on the event. For a more relaxed vibe, head to Skandinavian Bar, one of the oldest bars in Mykonos Town. This casual spot offers a mix of classic cocktails, friendly service, and an energetic atmosphere, making it a great place to meet new people. Drinks usually cost around €10-€15.

For a quieter yet equally enjoyable night out, Ano Mera, a peaceful village on the island, offers a more laid-back approach to nightlife. Here, you'll find local tavernas serving up fresh seafood and traditional Greek dishes, where you can enjoy a leisurely dinner under the stars. Kiki's Tavern, located near Agios Sostis Beach, is famous for its grilled meats and rustic charm, and it's a perfect place to enjoy a meal with a more intimate ambiance. Prices typically range from €15 to €25 per person for a meal.

In Paros, the nightlife is a bit more relaxed but still lively, especially in Naoussa and Parikia. Naoussa, the island's most vibrant town, has a wide range of bars and clubs that stay open late into the night. Sante Club, located near the harbor, is one of the most popular nightclubs, offering a mix of house and electronic music. The entrance fee typically ranges from €10 to €20, and the club often hosts themed parties and live performances. If you're after something more laid-back, head to Lageri Beach, where you'll find beach bars offering refreshing cocktails and chilled vibes. The Dubliner, a classic pub in Parikia, is a great spot for a more casual night out with live music and drinks. It's a fun place to mingle with both locals and tourists, and a pint of beer or cocktail costs around €5-€8.

On Naxos, the nightlife is more subdued but still enjoyable for those who like a relaxed evening out. Chora, the island's main town, has a variety of bars and cafes where you can enjoy a drink while watching the sunset over the Aegean Sea. Ippokampos Beach Bar is a great spot for sunset cocktails and light snacks. The laid-back atmosphere and stunning views make it a perfect spot for a more tranquil evening. For a bit of nightlife energy, check out Naxos Town's bars such as The Old Market Bar, where you can enjoy Greek music, and chat with friendly locals. Drinks here typically cost around €8-€12.

If you're looking for a more traditional Greek experience, Tinos offers a variety of venues where you can enjoy local entertainment. Tinos Town has plenty of tavernas with live Greek music, where locals gather to dance and sing. The atmosphere is festive but not overly commercialized, and you'll find a mix of folk music and contemporary hits played by local bands. The Panagia Evangelistria Festival, held every August 15th, is another highlight for those visiting during the summer. It's a religious celebration, but it's also a time for communal dancing, music, and feasting in the streets. You'll find bars in Tinos Town serving local wine and cocktails, with drinks averaging around €8-€12.

On Ios, the nightlife is geared toward a younger crowd, with lively beach bars and clubs offering a fun and energetic atmosphere. Ios Town (also known as Chora) is home to some of the most famous bars and clubs in the Cyclades. The Far Out Club is one of the island's most popular spots, known for its beach parties and guest DJs. The club is open late and plays an eclectic mix of house, electronic, and pop music, drawing large crowds in the summer months. The entrance fee usually ranges from €10 to €20, depending on the event. For a more casual evening, head to The Souvlaki Bar in Ios Town, where you can enjoy great food and an easygoing atmosphere before heading to one of the island's late-night venues. Ios is also famous for its beach bars, like Mylopotas Beach Bar, which offers a lively beach party vibe and a perfect place to dance by the water. The drinks here are reasonably priced, starting at around €7 for a cocktail.

Kea, a quieter island, offers a more laid-back nightlife experience with fewer nightclubs and bars. However, the small towns like Ioulis and Korissia offer a few charming tavernas and bars where you can relax and unwind after a day of hiking or exploring. The tavernas often host live music sessions, particularly during the summer months. These informal performances focus on traditional Greek songs, and the atmosphere is welcoming and authentic. Kea's nightlife is more about enjoying the evening with friends and family over great food, rather than high-energy clubs, making it ideal for those looking for a more peaceful night out.

For those visiting Folegandros, the island's nightlife scene is peaceful and intimate, making it perfect for a relaxing evening. The village of Chora offers several quaint bars and cafes, perfect for enjoying a quiet drink while taking in the stunning views of the Aegean Sea. Folegandros Town Square is a popular spot in the evening, where locals gather to enjoy ice cream, share a coffee, or sip on traditional Greek beverages. The island's small tavernas often feature live Greek music, creating a festive yet serene atmosphere that suits families or couples looking for a more relaxed night out. Dining and drinks typically cost between €15 and €25 per person.

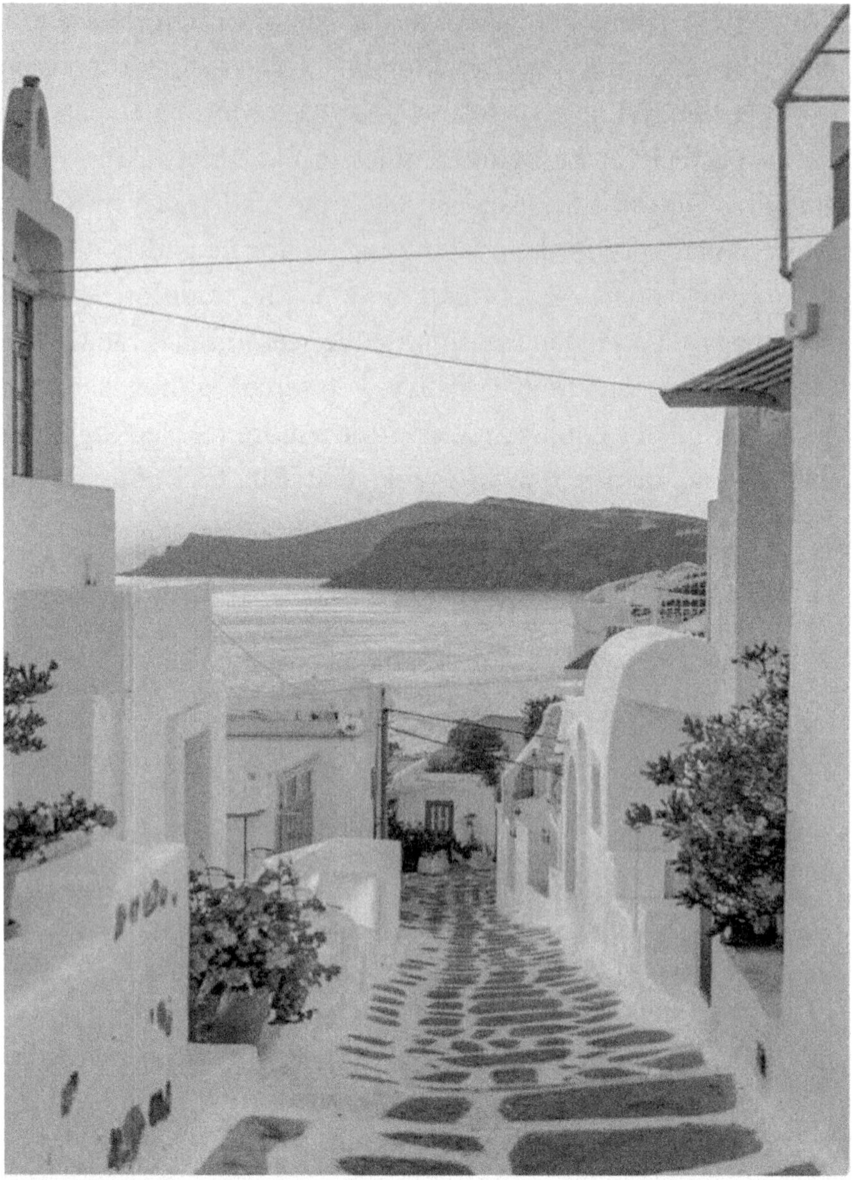

Food & Drink

Local Cuisine

The Cyclades offer a rich tapestry of local cuisine, deeply rooted in tradition and influenced by the islands' natural bounty. The food here is fresh, simple, and flavorful, with many dishes showcasing the region's agricultural and maritime heritage. Each island has its own unique twist on classic Greek cuisine, offering a delightful array of flavors that are perfect for food lovers looking to explore authentic local tastes.

On Naxos, one of the most famous culinary ingredients is the island's graviera cheese, a semi-hard cheese made from sheep's milk. The cheese has a rich, nutty flavor and is often served as an appetizer or used in traditional dishes like sagani, a baked dish made with graviera, eggs, and herbs. You'll find it in almost every taverna, with many restaurants offering it as part of a larger meze platter. A great place to try Naxian graviera is To Elliniko, located in Chora (Naxos Town), which is known for its traditional Greek fare and warm atmosphere. Expect to pay around €12 for a platter of local cheeses, including the famous graviera.

Another Naxian specialty is kavourmas, a spiced pork dish traditionally prepared in the winter months. The pork is marinated in olive oil, garlic, and various herbs before being slow-cooked. It's often served with bread, and in some places, you'll find it as part of a larger platter of cold cuts. A favorite spot to try this dish is La Vigne, a cozy restaurant in Chora that serves classic Naxian dishes. Meals here generally cost between €15 and €25 per person, with generous portions and fresh, local ingredients.

On Paros, the cuisine reflects the island's proximity to the sea, with an abundance of seafood dishes. Grilled octopus, a quintessential dish of the Cyclades, is commonly served as a meze, often accompanied by a side of fava—a smooth, creamy dip made from split peas. Fava is a staple across the islands, and on Paros, it is particularly celebrated for its creamy texture and delicate flavor. One of the best places to try these dishes is Taverna Glafkos, located in Naoussa, where fresh fish and seafood are the star of the menu. A typical seafood meal at Glafkos, with grilled octopus and fava, will cost between €20 and €30 per person, depending on your order.

For something more filling, Paros is also known for its hearty moussaka, a baked dish layered with minced meat, potatoes, and béchamel sauce. Many tavernas serve this comfort food, but To Pefko, also in Naoussa, is one of the best spots for a satisfying, traditional serving of moussaka. Expect to pay about €15 to €20 for a generous portion, often paired with a refreshing glass of local wine.

Mykonos may be famous for its lively nightlife, but its cuisine is no less impressive. The island is known for its kopanisti, a spicy cheese made from sheep or goat milk. The cheese is soft, tangy, and perfect as a spread on fresh bread or as part of a meze platter. You can find it in many tavernas across Mykonos, and a great place to sample it is Katerina's Taverna in Mykonos Town. The cost for a small serving of kopanisti with bread is around €7 to €10. Mykonos is also known for its louza, a local cured pork product that's often sliced thin and served with a side of olives. For a more substantial meal, Mamma's Taverna in Mykonos Town offers delicious souvlaki (grilled skewers of meat), often served with a fresh salad and a side of yogurt. A typical meal here costs around €15 to €20.

For something lighter, Mykonos' proximity to the sea makes it an excellent place for fresh seafood, and Kalafatis Beach offers a number of seafood restaurants where grilled fish and shellfish are served fresh from the Aegean. One such place is Nikolas Taverna, located near the beach, where you can enjoy grilled fish, shrimp, and lobster spaghetti. A meal for two here typically costs between €40 and €50, depending on the selection.

On Tinos, the cuisine draws heavily from the island's agricultural roots, with a focus on locally grown vegetables, legumes, and sheep's milk products. One dish you must try is revithada, a chickpea stew slow-cooked in a traditional clay pot. It's hearty and filling, often made with onions, olive oil, and a variety of herbs. The dish is typically served at most tavernas on Tinos, and a great place to sample it is Taverna Michalis, located in Tinos Town. Meals here generally cost around €12 to €18 per person, and you'll often find revithada as part of a larger meze platter.

Tinos is also known for its local honey, which has a distinct flavor due to the island's diverse flora. The honey is often used in desserts or drizzled over local cheeses. Tinos Honey Shop, located in the village of Kardiani, is the place to go for a variety of honey-based products, including honeycomb and honey-infused liqueurs. A jar of local honey costs around €10 to €15, depending on the size.

In Ios, one of the island's specialties is kreatopita, a meat pie made with ground lamb or pork, mixed with herbs and spices, and baked in a flaky pastry. It's a comforting, savory dish that's often served as part of a meze spread. You can try kreatopita at Katogi in Chora, Ios' main town, where traditional Greek dishes are the focus. The cost for a generous portion of kreatopita is around €12 to €15.

Folegandros, though smaller than its neighboring islands, offers delightful dishes with a focus on fresh, local ingredients. The island's food is known for its simplicity and its use of local herbs and olive oil. One dish you'll want to try is fava, a mashed split pea dip, which is often served as a starter in many tavernas. Folegandros is also famous for its local cheeses, which are made from sheep's milk and offer a rich, earthy flavor. Chora, the island's main town, has a number of charming tavernas where you can enjoy a simple meal of fava and local cheese, paired with a glass of wine. A meal for two typically costs around €25 to €30.

Best Tavernas

The Cyclades are known for their rich culinary traditions, and one of the best ways to experience the authentic flavors of the islands is by dining in the local tavernas. These charming, often family-run establishments offer a taste of Greek hospitality, where fresh ingredients, time-honored recipes, and a relaxed atmosphere come together to create unforgettable dining experiences. From cozy spots tucked away in villages to seaside tavernas with stunning views, the Cyclades have no shortage of exceptional places to enjoy traditional Greek cuisine.

In Mykonos, the taverna scene is as diverse as the island itself. Kiki's Tavern, located near Agios Sostis Beach, is a must-visit for anyone looking for a laid-back dining experience. This rustic spot, set in a peaceful corner of the island, serves simple yet delicious Greek dishes, such as grilled meats, fresh seafood, and the famous Greek salad. There's no menu here – the offerings change daily based on what's fresh and in season, but whatever you order, you'll be treated to mouthwatering dishes made with local ingredients. Expect to pay around €15 to €25 per person for a meal, and don't forget to try their famous saganaki (fried cheese). The taverna opens for lunch and dinner, usually from 12:00 PM to 6:00 PM, and it's best to arrive early, as it gets quite busy.

In Tinos, Taverna Michalis is a gem known for its authentic Tinian flavors. Located in Tinos Town, this family-run taverna is famous for its hearty louza (cured pork) and kavourmas (spiced pork), both local specialties. The meat is slow-cooked and served alongside fresh bread and local cheeses. The warm, rustic atmosphere of the taverna, with its friendly owners and traditional Greek décor, makes it a welcoming spot for both locals and tourists. Meals at Taverna Michalis typically cost between €15 and €25 per person, and the taverna is open daily from 12:00 PM to 11:00 PM. Be sure to try the local Tinos wine, which pairs perfectly with the food.

On Paros, Taverna Glafkos in Naoussa is a beloved spot for those wanting to experience the freshest seafood in a relaxed yet stylish setting. Situated by the water, this taverna offers sweeping views of the harbor and is known for its grilled octopus, fresh fish, and fava (split pea puree). The taverna is a perfect place to enjoy a leisurely meal with the sound of the sea in the background. Dishes here range from €20 to €30 per person, with a variety of options from appetizers to mains. Taverna Glafkos is open daily for lunch and dinner, from 12:00 PM to 10:00 PM, and it's a fantastic spot to soak in the atmosphere while savoring authentic local flavors.

For a truly authentic experience in Naxos, To Kastro in Chora is a family-run taverna that showcases the island's rich agricultural traditions. Known for its revithada (chickpea stew) and kouneli stifado (rabbit stew), To Kastro offers dishes made from local ingredients, including Naxian potatoes and cheese. The taverna's cozy atmosphere, combined with its delicious, rustic meals, makes it a great spot for a laid-back dinner with friends or family. Meals here typically range from €15 to €25 per person. To Kastro is open from 12:00 PM to 10:00 PM daily, and you'll be treated to some of the best Naxian comfort food on the island.

Ios is home to many charming tavernas, but one of the standout spots is Katogi in Chora. This taverna is known for its traditional Greek dishes, including kreatopita (meat pie), moussaka, and souvlaki. The warm ambiance, with its rustic wooden tables and family-friendly vibe, makes it a perfect place to enjoy a hearty meal. Dishes here typically cost between €10 and €20 per person, and the taverna is open daily from 12:00 PM to 10:00 PM. Katogi also has an impressive wine list, featuring local wines that perfectly complement the meal.

On Folegandros, Taverna Pireos is a hidden gem that offers an authentic taste of island life. Located in the village of Chora, this taverna is beloved by locals for its home-cooked meals and relaxed atmosphere. Folegandros is known for its fresh, simple cuisine, and Taverna Pireos serves up dishes like fava (split pea dip), grilled fish, and lamb in wine sauce. The portions are generous, and the ingredients are all sourced locally, making for a truly authentic dining experience. A meal here typically costs between €15 and €25 per person. The taverna is open from 12:00 PM to 10:00 PM daily, offering an ideal place to enjoy a leisurely meal after a day of exploring.

In Kea, Taverna Kouneni in the village of Ioulis is a wonderful spot to experience traditional Greek flavors in a cozy, village setting. Known for its moussaka, souvlaki, and local cheese pies, the taverna is a favorite among locals and visitors alike. The warm, welcoming atmosphere and friendly service make it a great place to relax with family or friends. Meals at Taverna Kouneni typically cost around €15 to €20 per person, and the taverna is open daily from 12:00 PM to 11:00 PM.

Wine & Spirits

The Cyclades offer a wine and spirits experience that reflects the islands' deep connection to their land and history. These islands have been producing wine for centuries, and their local varieties, often unique to the region, are a testament to the islands' ancient agricultural traditions. The Cycladic islands also offer a variety of spirits, including raki and ouzo, both of which play an important role in Greek culture and hospitality. Whether you're sipping a glass of wine in a seaside taverna or sampling local spirits with a meze, the Cyclades offer a rich and authentic taste of Greek beverages.

Naxos, the largest island in the Cyclades, is particularly well-known for its wine. The island's volcanic soil and warm climate make it ideal for growing grapes, and Naxos has a long history of wine production. Naxian wine is typically made from a variety of local grapes, with Mavrotragano (a red variety) and Assyrtiko (a white variety) being the most prominent. The wine is known for its full-bodied, rich flavor, and there are many small wineries on the island where visitors can sample and purchase local varieties. Domaine Karamolegos, located near the village of Sangri, is one of the best wineries on Naxos. This family-run winery offers tours of the vineyards, where you can learn about the island's winemaking process, followed by a tasting of their signature wines. Prices for wine tastings typically range from €10 to €20 per person, and the winery is open daily from 10:00 AM to 6:00 PM. It's a great way to experience the island's terroir while learning about Naxos' wine culture.

On Paros, the wine culture is also thriving, with local wineries producing some excellent wines. The island is known for its white wines made from the Monemvasia grape variety, which is unique to the Cyclades. These wines are light, crisp, and often have citrus notes, making them the perfect complement to the island's fresh seafood. One of the top wineries to visit on Paros is Moraitis Winery, located near Naoussa. The winery offers tours of its cellars and vineyards, and visitors can sample a variety of wines, including their famous white Monemvasia and rich red Agiorgitiko. Wine tastings at Moraitis Winery typically cost between €15 and €20 per person, and the winery is open daily from 10:00 AM to 7:00 PM. The beautiful location and informative tours make this winery a must-visit for wine lovers.

Tinos is another island in the Cyclades that has a growing wine culture. While the island is often associated with its religious significance and traditional architecture, it's also home to some fantastic wineries that produce exceptional local wines. The most notable wine from Tinos is Tinian Assyrtiko, a crisp, dry white wine that pairs beautifully with seafood dishes. Tinos Wine Cooperative is a great place to sample a variety of local wines and learn about the island's winemaking traditions. The cooperative offers wine tastings, and you can also purchase bottles of their wines to take home. The tasting experience costs around €10 to €15 per person, and the cooperative is open daily from 9:00 AM to 3:00 PM. Tinos' combination of volcanic soil and Mediterranean climate gives its wines a distinctive character, and visiting the cooperative is a great way to dive into the island's rich vinous heritage.

In Mykonos, the wine scene may not be as famous as on some of the other islands, but the island still has a selection of excellent local wines, many of which are perfect for pairing with seafood. The island is known for its production of local white wines and rosé, which are typically made from indigenous Greek grape varieties. While Mykonos is better known for its cosmopolitan atmosphere and vibrant nightlife, several upscale restaurants and tavernas feature local wines, along with imported varieties from mainland Greece and other regions. Avli, located in Mykonos Town, offers a wonderful selection of Greek wines, and the ambiance is perfect for enjoying a glass while people-watching. Expect to pay around €10-€20 per glass for local wine, with the restaurant open daily from 12:00 PM to 12:00 AM.

In addition to wine, the Cyclades are home to some of Greece's most iconic spirits. Ouzo, the anise-flavored liquor, is perhaps the most famous of Greek spirits and is a staple of island life. It's typically served as an aperitif, accompanied by a small plate of meze (small dishes) such as olives, cheese, and grilled seafood. On Tinos, you can sample the island's own version of ouzo, which is distilled locally and often served with a splash of water. Local ouzo is available in many tavernas, and prices typically range from €2 to €5 per glass.

Another popular spirit in the Cyclades is raki, a strong grape-based spirit similar to rakija, which is commonly consumed in the islands during festive occasions. Raki is particularly popular on Crete, but it is also enjoyed in the Cyclades. On Paros, raki is often offered as a welcome drink at local tavernas, and it's common to be served after a meal, especially during family gatherings or celebrations. The drink is often accompanied by a slice of cheese or a sweet pastry. The cost for a glass of raki typically ranges from €2 to €4.

In Ios, the local distillery produces mastiha, a unique spirit made from the resin of the mastic tree, which is native to the nearby island of Chios. Mastiha has a sweet, herbal flavor and is often used in cocktails or sipped neat as a digestif. Ios Mastiha Distillery offers tastings of this distinctive spirit, allowing visitors to explore the different variations of mastiha.

Tasting sessions typically cost around €5 to €10 per person, and the distillery is open daily from 9:00 AM to 5:00 PM.

Cooking Classes

The Cyclades offer an exceptional culinary journey, and one of the best ways to truly understand the islands' food culture is by taking a cooking class. Whether you're an experienced cook or just looking to try something new, the islands provide an opportunity to immerse yourself in the local food traditions. From preparing fresh seafood to learning the secrets behind beloved Greek comfort foods, cooking classes in the Cyclades allow you to take a piece of the island home with you—one recipe at a time.

In Paros, cooking enthusiasts can head to Paros Cooking Classes, located in the picturesque village of Naoussa. Here, you'll have the chance to learn traditional Greek cooking techniques in an intimate, hands-on setting. The class focuses on local specialties, and you'll be taught how to prepare dishes like revithada (chickpea stew), fresh seafood, and fava (split pea puree), all using the island's fresh, local ingredients. The class is designed for all skill levels, so whether you're a beginner or a seasoned cook, you'll be able to follow along with ease. After preparing your dishes, you'll sit down to enjoy your meal, often accompanied by a glass of local wine.

The cost for a half-day class ranges from €60 to €80 per person, and the classes typically last 3 to 4 hours. They are available from May to October, but it's best to book in advance, especially during peak season.

Over on Naxos, Naxos Cooking School offers an authentic taste of the island's culinary heritage. Local chef Niki invites visitors into her kitchen to learn the art of Naxian cooking. The island's cuisine is deeply connected to its land, and dishes like kouneli stifado (rabbit stew) and souvlaki showcase the abundance of fresh produce and local meats. You'll also learn to make traditional Greek staples like moussaka and tzatziki, and Niki takes great care to explain the history behind each dish and its significance on the island. Classes are small, intimate, and highly interactive, providing a hands-on experience with all the ingredients sourced from Naxos itself. The cost for a class is around €50 to €70 per person, and the class lasts for about 3 hours. Naxos Cooking School is open year-round, and it's a fantastic way to learn authentic recipes that you can recreate back home.

Mykonos, famous for its glamorous nightlife, also offers a culinary experience that reflects the island's Mediterranean and Greek roots. Mykonos Cooking Class offers cooking workshops where you can learn to prepare the island's fresh seafood dishes, such as grilled octopus, sea bass with lemon and herbs, and lobster pasta. These dishes highlight Mykonos' proximity to the sea, and the cooking class focuses on using fresh, seasonal ingredients to create simple yet flavorful meals. In addition to seafood, you'll also master Greek classics like spanakopita (spinach pie) and dolmades (stuffed grape leaves). The class ends with a meal, where you can enjoy the fruits of your labor. Classes cost between €75 and €100 per person, and each class lasts about 3 hours. They are available year-round, but it's best to book early, especially during the busy summer months.

For something uniquely Tinian, Tinos Cooking Class offers an immersive experience that takes you into the heart of the island's food culture. The island's cuisine is heavily influenced by its rich agricultural landscape, with dishes based on locally sourced ingredients like olives, cheese, and herbs. At Tinos Cooking Class, you'll learn how to prepare Tinian specialties such as louza (cured pork), revithada (chickpea stew), and kavourmas (spiced pork preserve). The cooking class is held in a traditional Tinian kitchen, where you can experience the island's rural charm and learn about the island's culinary traditions. A typical class lasts about 3 hours and costs between €50 and €75 per person. The school is open from May to October, and reservations are recommended.

In Ios, Ios Cooking School offers a more casual but equally rewarding cooking experience. The island's culinary scene is centered around simple, fresh ingredients, with a focus on seafood and traditional Greek fare. Here, you'll have the chance to learn how to prepare dishes such as kreatopita (meat pie), moussaka, and souvlaki, along with a variety of meze (small appetizers). The classes are tailored to suit a variety of skill levels, making them an excellent option for both beginners and more experienced cooks. The cost for a class is around €60 per person, and the class typically lasts 3 hours. The school is open from April to October, and it's ideal for anyone wanting to learn how to make classic Greek dishes with a local twist.

On Kea, a quieter and more rustic island, you can take part in private cooking lessons where you'll be guided through the process of preparing traditional Greek meals using fresh, locally grown ingredients. Kea Cooking Classes are tailored to suit small groups or families and offer a more personalized experience. You'll learn to prepare simple but delicious dishes like moussaka, feta pie, and baklava, all while exploring the island's food culture. Classes are available upon request, and prices start at €100 for 2-3 people. These private sessions typically last between 3 to 4 hours, and it's a great way to immerse yourself in the flavors of Kea in an intimate, hands-on environment.

The Cyclades also offer more casual cooking experiences, such as taverna cooking demonstrations where local chefs showcase how to prepare regional dishes. These events allow you to learn about traditional Greek cooking methods while enjoying a relaxed meal in the heart of the islands. Many tavernas across the Cyclades offer these informal cooking lessons, often featuring local specialties like souvlaki, grilled fish, and moussaka. Prices for cooking demonstrations typically range from €20 to €40 per person, depending on the taverna and the type of meal prepared.

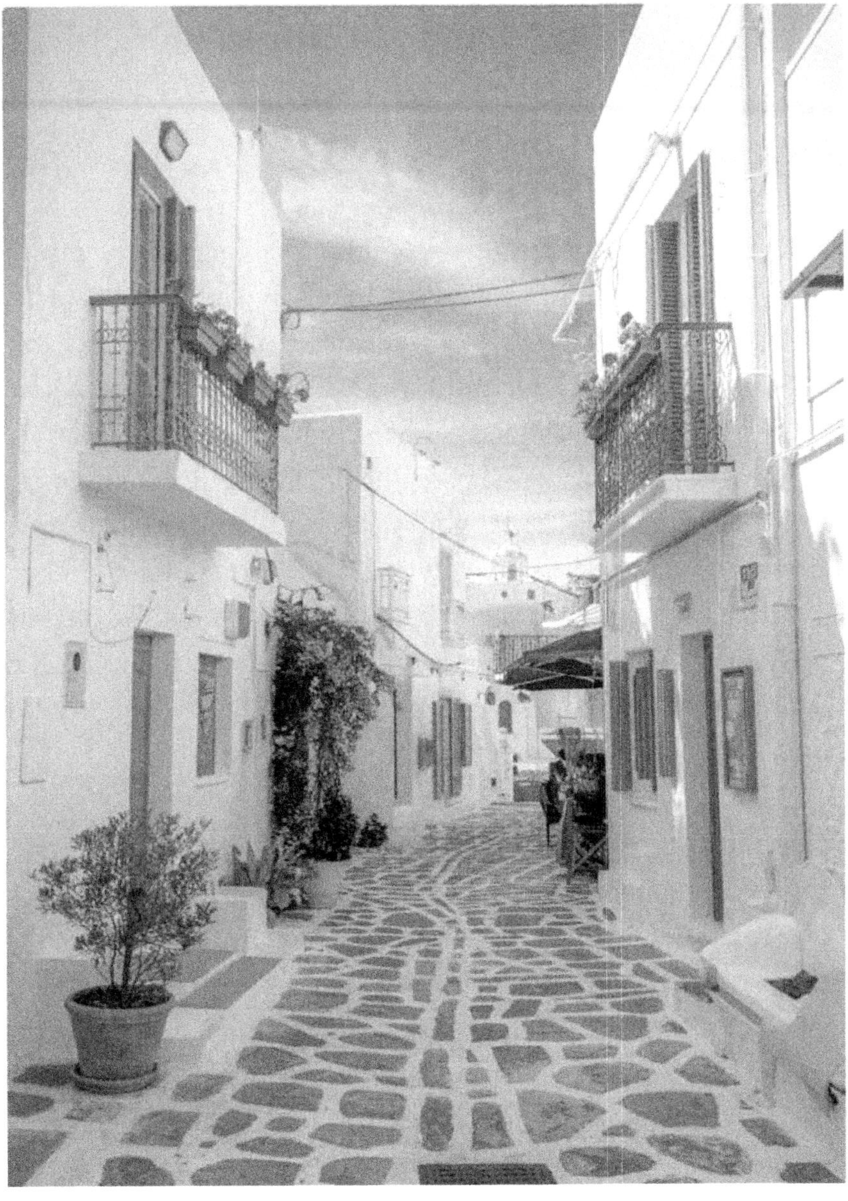

Practical Information

Packing Guide

When planning a trip to the Cyclades, packing wisely ensures you have everything you need to enjoy the islands to the fullest. The weather in the Cyclades can be quite variable, with warm summers and mild winters, so packing for a variety of conditions is essential. For the summer months, lightweight clothing is a must. Think breathable fabrics like cotton and linen, which will keep you cool and comfortable while exploring the islands. A few pairs of shorts, light dresses, T-shirts, and tank tops will be your go-to items for daytime activities. Evenings can be a little cooler, so a light jacket or cardigan is a good idea, especially if you're planning to dine outside near the sea, where the breeze can feel chilly.

Good quality swimwear is a must, as the Cyclades are famous for their stunning beaches. Pack at least two swimsuits so you can rotate them throughout the trip. If you plan on spending time hiking, exploring villages, or visiting archaeological sites, comfortable walking shoes are essential. Opt for sturdy sandals or sneakers, as the terrain can be uneven in some areas, particularly if you're walking along cobblestone streets or to remote beaches.

For excursions, a daypack is useful for carrying essentials like water, sunscreen, a hat, and a camera. Sunscreen is a must, as the sun in the Cyclades can be intense, especially in the summer months. Bring high SPF lotion or spray to protect your skin, as well as lip balm with SPF. A wide-brimmed hat or a cap will also keep you shaded and protected. If you plan to do any water activities like snorkeling, kayaking, or paddleboarding, consider bringing waterproof bags or pouches to keep your belongings safe.

If you're visiting during the off-season or early spring and fall, the weather can be milder, but still unpredictable. You'll want to bring a lightweight jacket, perhaps a sweater for the evenings, and closed shoes for cooler days. While most of the islands have great weather for sightseeing year-round, some might experience rain, so a foldable rain jacket or a small, compact umbrella can come in handy.

When it comes to accessories, don't forget sunglasses to protect your eyes from the sun's glare, especially if you're spending time outdoors or near the water. A camera or smartphone with plenty of memory is also a good idea to capture the island's stunning landscapes, architecture, and sunsets. If you're planning to visit monasteries or churches, make sure to pack clothing that covers your shoulders and knees, as these are required for entry.

For personal items, bring any medications you might need, especially if you have specific prescriptions, as pharmacies can be limited in smaller villages. A travel adapter for charging your electronics is also crucial, as the electrical outlets in Greece may differ from those in your home country.

Lastly, if you plan on visiting any upscale restaurants or bars, pack a nicer outfit for evening wear, such as a nice dress or a collared shirt. Although the islands are generally laid-back, there are some venues that may have a more refined dress code. Also, if you're someone who likes to try the local wines, bringing back a bottle or two as souvenirs is easy, as the Cyclades are known for their excellent wine production.

Budgeting Advice

When preparing a trip to the Cyclades, it's important to budget carefully to ensure a smooth and enjoyable vacation, as the islands cater to a range of budgets, from affordable backpacker experiences to high-end luxury stays. The key to balancing costs lies in knowing where to allocate funds for accommodation, food, activities, and transportation.

Accommodation costs in the Cyclades vary widely depending on the island, the time of year, and the type of accommodation. Islands like Santorini and Mykonos tend to be more expensive, especially during peak tourist season (from June to September). For a mid-range hotel or boutique stay, you can expect to pay between €150 and €500+ per night. If you're on a tighter budget, there are still affordable options, such as hostels or guesthouses, where you can find rooms starting at around €40-€80 per night. For cheaper alternatives, islands like Naxos, Paros, and Ios generally offer more budget-friendly accommodation. You'll find a variety of options ranging from simple rooms to mid-range hotels, typically priced between €30 and €80 per night.

Food is an essential part of the Cycladic experience, but dining costs can vary depending on where you are. Santorini and Mykonos are known for their upscale dining scenes, and meals at mid-range restaurants can cost around €20-€40 per person. However, if you're on a budget, the iconic Greek gyros or souvlaki are delicious and affordable options, typically priced between €3 and €7 for a quick, satisfying meal. On islands like Paros, Naxos, and Tinos, food is more reasonably priced. A meal at a mid-range taverna typically costs between €10-€20 per person, and you can also save by visiting local markets to pick up fresh produce for self-catering. Greek meze (small plates) are also a great way to enjoy a variety of dishes without spending too much. If you're looking to save on meals, self-catering or grabbing street food are great ways to cut costs.

Transportation between the islands is another factor to consider in your budget. Ferries are the most common way to travel between the islands, with prices fluctuating depending on the distance, ferry type, and season. A one-way ferry ticket can range from €20 to €50 per person. Mykonos and Santorini typically have more expensive and frequent ferry routes due to their popularity. If you plan on exploring more remote islands, the cost of ferries could add up, so consider booking tickets in advance to secure better prices.

Once on the islands, getting around is relatively affordable. Local buses on the islands are an excellent way to explore, with tickets generally priced between €1-€3 per ride. Renting a scooter or a car can also be a budget-friendly option, especially if you're traveling in a group and want to visit beaches and villages at your own pace. Expect to pay around €20-€40 per day for a scooter rental, and between €40-€70 for a car rental, depending on the type of vehicle.

Activities and excursions vary greatly in cost. If you're looking to explore the islands' natural beauty, hiking trails, and free public beaches, many of these activities won't cost you anything. A visit to archaeological sites or museums might have an entry fee of €3-€10, while boat trips and organized tours tend to be priced between €25-€50 per person, depending on the tour length and destination. To save on activities, consider exploring on foot or using public transport rather than booking expensive guided tours.

Emergency Contacts

When traveling to the Cyclades, it's important to be prepared in case of an emergency. Knowing the key contacts and local services can make all the difference should something unexpected arise. The islands are generally safe and well-equipped, but having access to emergency numbers and important resources will help ensure peace of mind during your trip.

For general emergencies, the European emergency number 112 works across the Cyclades, including medical, fire, and police emergencies. This number is free to call and can be dialed from any phone, whether it's a mobile or landline.

For medical emergencies, the primary contact is the National Emergency Center (EKAV). You can reach their ambulance service by calling 166. EKAV operates throughout Greece and will send a medical team if necessary. Major islands, including Mykonos, Santorini, and Naxos, have local hospitals where you can receive care. Mykonos General Hospital, located in the town of Mykonos, is equipped to handle a range of medical issues. Similarly, Santorini Hospital in Fira and Naxos Hospital in Chora provide comprehensive care for visitors. For minor medical issues, many islands have local pharmacies, with pharmacy hours usually running from

9:00 AM to 2:00 PM and 5:00 PM to 8:00 PM, though some may vary slightly.

For police emergencies, you can reach the Greek Police by calling 100, and they can assist with anything from lost property to more serious issues. Every island has a local police station, and larger islands like Mykonos and Santorini have 24-hour police services. Smaller islands typically have a police presence during regular working hours but may have limited staff after hours.

If you're in need of consular assistance, it's a good idea to contact the nearest embassy or consulate. For U.S. citizens, the U.S. Embassy in Athens can provide support for issues such as lost passports, legal matters, or other emergencies. The embassy's contact number is +30 210 720 2490, and for urgent matters, +30 210 729 4444 (after hours). Similarly, travelers from other countries can refer to their respective embassies or consulates for support.

For lost or stolen property, your first stop should be the police station to report the issue. If you lose your passport or important documents, it's essential to notify your embassy or consulate right away to ensure they can issue replacements or provide guidance.

It's also a good idea to have local taxi services and transportation contacts handy, especially if you're in an emergency situation where quick transport is necessary. Taxis are available on most islands, with local numbers easily found on hotel reception desks or through your accommodation.

If you have a medical condition or require specific assistance, it's recommended to bring along a travel insurance policy that includes coverage for medical emergencies. Ensure that you have the insurance details easily accessible, and know how to reach your insurance provider in case of emergency. Many health insurance companies offer emergency contact numbers for abroad, which can be vital for treatment in the Cyclades.

Greek Phrases

Learning a few key phrases in Greek can greatly enhance your experience in the Cyclades, as it allows you to connect with locals and shows respect for their culture. While many Greeks in the islands speak English, especially in tourist areas, a few words in Greek will certainly be appreciated. Here are some useful phrases to get you started:

Basic Greetings and Polite Expressions
Hello – Yia sou (informal) / Yia sas (formal)
Good morning – Kalimera
Good evening – Kalispera
Good night – Kalinichta
Goodbye – Antio
Please – Parakalo
Thank you – Efharisto
You're welcome – Parakalo (also used for "please")
Excuse me / Sorry – Signomi
Yes – Nai
No – Ochi

Useful Phrases for Traveling
How much is this? – Poso kanei afto?
Where is...? – Pou einai...?
I need help – Chreiazomai voitheia

I don't understand – Den katalaveno
Can you speak English? – Milate Anglika?
I'm lost – Exo xafnistei
Is it far? – Einai makria?
What time does it open? – Ti ora anoigei?
What time does it close? – Ti ora klistai?
I would like... – Thelo...

Shopping and Dining
How much is this? – Poso kanei afto?
I would like to buy... – Thelo na agoraso...
Menu – Karta
Water – Nero
Wine – Krasí
Beer – Bira
A table for two, please – Enan trapezi gia dio, parakalo
The bill, please – Ton logariasmo, parakalo

Emergencies
Help! – Voitheia!
Call the police – Pate na prokalesete tin astynomia
I need a doctor – Chreiazomai foritro
Where is the hospital? – Pou einai to nosokomio?
I am sick – Eimai arrostos

.

Numbers (1-10)
1 – Ena
2 – Dyo
3 – Tria
4 – Tesseris
5 – Pente
6 – Exi
7 – Epta
8 – Ocho
9 – Ennea
10 – Deka

conclusion

The Cyclades offer a rich and diverse experience, where every island tells its own unique story. From the striking white-washed buildings of Santorini and Mykonos to the peaceful charm of Naxos, Paros, and Ios, each island has something special to offer, whether it's breathtaking landscapes, rich history, delicious cuisine, or vibrant local culture. The beauty of the Cyclades lies in its balance – the serenity of the quieter islands perfectly complements the lively energy of the more popular destinations.

As you've explored this guide, I hope it has inspired you to not only visit the Cyclades but to fully immerse yourself in its way of life. Whether you're savoring traditional dishes in a seaside taverna, hiking to ancient ruins, or lounging on sun-drenched beaches, the Cyclades will undoubtedly leave a lasting impression. Every corner of this stunning archipelago invites you to slow down, experience the local hospitality, and create memories that will stay with you long after you've left.

Printed in Great Britain
by Amazon